THE END OF ALL WORRIES:

WE ARE ALL ONE

Scientific and Spiritual Testimonies
to the Unity of All Things

By Irie Glajar

Cover design: Irie Glajar and David Walker

Published by Positive Imaging, LLC
9016 Palace Parkway
Austin, TX 78748
http://positive-imaging.com

ISBN: 978-0-9842480-2-5

Printed in the United States of America

No tree is so foolish as to have its own branches fight among themselves.

Native American wisdom

To my son, my wife, my sister, my mother, and my father: thank you for the inspiration and motivation to write this book.

Table of Contents

Foreword

There is a well known saying: if you want to feed a person for a day, give the person a fish; if you want to feed a person for life, teach the person how to fish. This implies that with our noble intent to do good deeds we should teach for life and not for a day, a month, or a year. However, how does one teach for life? Such teaching, whether the academic teaching or any other teaching-learning experience, must focus primarily on the meaning of what is being taught in the larger scheme of the universe. This endeavor not only needs a clear understanding of the world around us, but also requires both teacher and learner to understand their particular role in that larger picture. This is exactly the area in which religion, spirituality, and modern education in the West, under the present paradigm of separation, lack depth and completeness, which explains negative behavior. I find, therefore, that we should do whatever it takes to expand our understanding of the world, such that crime not only becomes pointless, but that human consciousness begins to guide generation after generation into territories of unheard of peace, constructive explorations, and love for life. This book is one more brick in the solid wall of such applied knowledge.

Once we understand the true position religion, spirituality, and education occupy in the formation of a human being, we will be able to assimilate those constructive messages that richly transpire from this kind of work. As soon as education begins teaching the larger picture of our position and our impact in the universe, we will see ourselves in a more meaningful light, which will implicitly affect our participation in the living body called Planet Earth. A common sense outcome of such a realization will automatically be that parents, relatives, friends, and even strangers will be directly interested in acting as true teachers and learners. Human individuals will not see themselves remotely separated from everything else including each other, but instead will realize that each person is a vital component and participant in the life of our planet, and therefore, as responsible for its well-being as anybody else.

Such a complex endeavor requires a more complete understanding of who we are and why our lives run the way they do. The basic ground should allow for the development of a human being capable of living at much higher ethical and moral standards.

We can consider this as a significant outcome that will take place in the lives of those who will seriously participate in the efforts to implement the new paradigm of union I am proposing in this book. We should expect such results to show up gradually over a period of time. Societies don't change over night, and it is even more difficult to change the widely accepted educational system. But considering that many times the human race has replaced existing beliefs with new ones, I am sure a shift for the better in the present educational model is possible. As with any other social change, this shift should start with the individual. Any human being can change personal perception of the world in an instance, given the proper motivational framework. I hope this book can provide such basis for change toward a better life for all of us.

Introduction

Life in the Western Hemisphere from the late 20th century and the early part of the 21st displays great technological, political, and cultural accomplishments. However, it shows little or no progress in other crucial areas of human development. This is easily observed in today's world by looking at what makes newspapers and television headlines. It is evident that many deep, spiritual human values are being sacrificed for selfish pursuits at both individual and international levels. We also need to take in consideration people's well-being from the medical point of view. A stronghold on conventional practices in medicine allows little or no progress in curing certain illnesses. Moreover, in spite of all technological development, crime motivated by anger, jealousy, and envy, continues to rise, and people of different social, spiritual, educational, and political backgrounds maintain self destructive practices.

As with anything else in the material world, where cause and effect is a basic law, this situation must have a cause. I believe the present educational model in the Western world is responsible for the aforementioned social trend. Since education in general has a definite impact on the quality of life, a shift in the existing educational paradigm at all levels must take place in order to offer hope for a positive and radical change in human behavior. The purpose of this book is to provide the necessary evidence as the foundation for a new educational paradigm, one capable of curing all the ills that obstruct real progress in our society. The core of this problem is challenged here by ancient and modern testimonies put forth by some of the greatest thinkers in the areas of science, religion, and spirituality. The problem lies mainly in a misunderstanding of the real nature of the universe and implicitly the place *we* have in it. The existing educational paradigm proclaims a separation between all material forms including human beings and it encourages the pursuit of happiness often at the direct expense of others.

The new model I present here is based on the union, connection, and interdependence of all that is, hence the unity of all living entities on Earth. This unity model proclaims that "We Are All

One," it is evidenced in ancient religious and spiritual writings, and it is finally supported by scientific breakthroughs of the last century, namely quantum physics. Research at the subatomic level also supports the well known movement in the medical field, which puts forth the theory of holistic treatment. This has been called era *two* and era *three* in medicine and is based on the non local nature of our universe and the reality of the universal union.

Throughout history, the spiritual masters have been offering a clear example of unity in the world and they maintain that the real values humans should treasure are nonmaterial in nature. These spiritual teachers suggest that we should make honesty, love, compassion, caring, patience, and understanding an integral part of our being. In other words, as the great teaching says, treat others as we would like to be treated. Implicitly, this approach gives us a solid reason for eliminating violence completely and to treasure high moral and ethical values. However, the philosophy of separation that stands at the foundation of the existing educational paradigm in the West fails to provide the inner incentive to follow unconditionally such high standards. The model I present here offers the needed common sense motivation for a major shift in general education: first as to the understanding of the universe, and second as to a new pattern in human behavior.

To support the new model, I will include some of my own experiences that convinced me of the universal connection and helped change my life for the better. Starting with the profound implication of my 1981 defection from Communist Romania, and after more mundane events in my personal and professional life, I learned that there is much more to the picture of being human than what we have been taught. Eventually, this road took me to a new model of thinking. The idea of the interconnection between all that is appeals to every approach I have considered: spiritual, religious, and scientific.

In order to facilitate the implementation of the new educational paradigm that pertains to all aspects of human life, I examine some important areas such as family relationship, religion, employment, entertainment, medicine, and academic education. As we consider exchanging negative behavior patterns for more constructive ones, I rely on the theoretical, experimental, and philosophical precepts advanced by an elite of great minds in science, religion, and spirituality.

I hope that throughout this book you, the readers, will keep an open mind to the possibilities that lay behind the reflections presented, and then draw your own conclusions as to the immediate practical and personal benefit of implementing such ideas in your own lives. I am certain that each one of us can contribute, in our own way, to the completion of the project I propose, namely the exchange of the existing philosophy of separation for the one of universal union. This is my chief pursuit and I am sure that this kind of philosophical shift in our perception of the world can eliminate all suffering inflicted by humans onto humans and onto nature at large. Consequently, we can reach "The End of all Worries."

Chapter 1:

The Problem

If we can really understand the problem,
the answer will come out of it,
because the answer is not separate from the problem.

Juddu Krishnamurti

Unresolved Social Issues

History often reveals negative trends in human behavior and these should be considered instructive for both the present and the future of our evolution. Although such lessons are evident when one focuses on sensitive issues concerning modern society, it is obvious that radical changes are seldom implemented for a positive impact on our life on Earth.

It is interesting to remember that "history repeats itself." With this in mind, let us explore a few well known historical facts that may provide a better understanding of some of today's main social concerns. Over millennia humans have made impressive discoveries with the primordial intention to ease their lives and to offer their families and community more security and prosperity. However, as this has been the main drive, there had always been a parallel, countervailing negative result. Here are some examples:

- Knife: This hunting instrument soon became a weapon against other human beings. The wide spread use of knives in a variety of crimes is very well documented.
- Fire: A positive revolution that continued human ascension throughout the ages. However, it is well known that fire has been and is being used also to destroy and kill.
- Gunpowder: The Chinese are renowned for taking humanity to a new realm of existence by inventing

gunpowder, but while explosives are used to build tunnels, they are also employed to kill and destroy.

- Automobile: The car was invented to serve our transportation needs, but simultaneously became a facilitator of war.
- Airplane: Traveling within hours between remote locations on Earth became possible with air travel, but at the same time it has greatly enhanced humans' capacity to destroy (the wars of the last hundred years and September 11, 2001 are a vivid memory).
- Nuclear bombs: Hiroshima and Nagasaki tragically remind us of probably the most important revolution in the modern era, when atomic energy was used first to destroy, but only later to produce electricity.
- Satellites: Since the 1950s artificial satellites and space exploration have expanded our horizon, but beside offering impressive possibilities in communication and the study of the Earth and the universe, they are being extensively employed as spying devices especially in war situations, therefore, facilitating more killing and destruction.
- Internet: While it should be applauded for providing fast communication between people, as well as offering access to libraries and information databases all over the world, we also must realize that the most searched word on the Internet is "sex," and most of the "searches" are done by teenagers. Illegal practices such as pedophilia and gambling are also greatly facilitated by the Internet and, as the daily news confirms, because of it, lost privacy and stolen identities are becoming major problems. Moreover, it should be noted that terrorists employ the Internet as well as anybody else.

Although we have just stepped into a new century and millennia, the atrocities that human beings bring upon human beings at a world-wide scale are at an all time high. The 20th century lays claim to some of the cruelest events in our history. The list includes, but is not limited to, the first and second World Wars, the vast cruelty of the Communist system all over the world, the Vietnam and the Korean Wars, mass killings in African countries, the ongoing conflicts in the Middle East, and of course the escalation of terrorist activities in many parts of the globe. Millions of people have been killed for political and material reasons, and many other millions have been forced to lives of suffering in desperation. If we add the most recent nuclear threat to this general picture of world-wide unrest, the somber possibility of a third world war becomes real.

On a smaller scale, let us consider the crimes committed within the borders of the United States. Acts of domestic violence that make the news would represent only the tip of the iceberg: husbands killing their wives, wives running their husbands over by car, parents badly mistreating their children, children shooting their parents, teenagers shooting schoolmates and teachers at school, police officers abusing their power on racial or gender grounds, priests sexually abusing church going teenagers, crimes based on sexual orientation, organized gangs, illegal drugs dealing, etc. As grave as this situation is, if we stay on this path there seems to be no real end in sight.

The wide spectrum of social concerns listed above is closely connected to the world's present educational system. Human behavior definitely depends on the core values assimilated by people within their respective societies. The existential model of union I propose in this book can offer the long searched for solution to most human problems.

Somber Statistics

There are three major areas of available statistical data to support my argument for a new educational model. The use of statistics is widespread in the modern world and such studies help us collect information that can contribute to major remedies in many sensitive areas. As I examine today's trends in the United States, existing data shows clearly that the path education took for many decades is not leading to the bright future we all want for the next generations.

First, let us examine some areas of major concern that are evidenced in the Statistical Abstract of the United States. This

National Data Book, published by the United States Department of
Commerce, Bureau of the Census, lists under the heading "Law
Enforcement, Courts, and Prisons," statistical tables on "Crime
Arrests and Victimizations," "Courts," "Juvenile, Child Abuse,"
"Prisoners and Inmates," and "Lawyers—Supreme Court." The
numbers describe an alarming situation in regard to the practical
implementation of basic moral and ethical values in the United
States:

Child Abuse and Neglect Cases Substantiated

Year:	1990	1993	1994	1995
Total:	690,658	966,163	1,011,595	1,000,502

Juvenile Arrests

Year:	1980	1995
Violent crime:	77,270	115,160
Drug abuse:	86,685	143,315

Prisoners and Inmates

Year:	1985	1995
Total:	256,615	507,044

Lawyers—Supreme Court

Year:	1960	1991
Total:	285,933	805,872

In recent years crime in the United States has still been on the
rise. Here is a glimpse of this situation from 2000 to 2003, respectively.

Murders, manslaughters (times 1000):
        15.6,   16.0,   16.2,   16.5.
Prisoners (times 1000):
        1,331,   1,345,   1,381,   1,409.

Even though these are just excerpts from the detailed Statistical Abstract, we can clearly see that the crime rate in the last few
decades has been generally on the rise. This fact concurs with grim
statistical reports made available by general media. Daily newspa-

pers, radio programs, and television news broadcasts provide us with continuous updates on such sad social realities. Human acts of an incredible violent nature make the headlines, which should raise deep concerns regarding the future of our children. Although one could argue that the crime increase can be correlated to the population increase over the years, the problem remains.

As we closely examine the general behavior around us, such discord manifests itself much more often than we would like. The numbers of well documented cases of child abuse and neglect are alarming. Over the past two decades the number of juvenile arrests due to violent crime and due to drug abuse has been increasing considerably.

Expanding on the study of unlawful behavior, the 1985–1995 decade, for example, shows an almost doubling of the number of prisoners and inmates. The iceberg metaphor suggests that in fact those who should have been prosecuted and eventually sentenced but were not, would most likely push this number even higher. Along these lines, in the first quarter of 1998, for example, an Austin television station sadly announced that Texas prisons were filled to maximum capacity, in many cases registering an overflow. As of 2004, the news is that the percentage of inmates in respect to the United States population is at an all-time high.

We in the West tend to focus on what needs to be fixed, versus on what is working well. We take "working well" for granted and we don't spend much time and energy praising it and/or improving it. The well known Western strategy to ensure a better future is to fix what is wrong, eliminating the negative. However, opening up to avenues that are more promising is a better strategy—for example, prevention can eliminate the need to fix at least some of the wrongs in our society.

Consequently, to enhance prevention, I propose a paradigm of union instead of the existing paradigm of separation. As soon as we understand that we are all one, united at a subatomic level, we will instinctively refrain from generating negativity. The first area of concern is ignoring the existing laws. Statistics on crime at all levels including invasion of others' legal and constitutional rights, are part of a wealth of evidence that points out the need for immediate cultural change. Standard education has the primary role to establish the norms for the next generation and should be the first area of public concern reevaluated under the proposed new educational model.

A second statistical area of interest is that of public opinion on issues concerning our day-by-day life. It is evident that people are inclined to pay more attention to entertainment than to deeper life concerns and cultural practices. Statistical studies done by prestigious educational institutions show that the population of tomorrow's parents, educators, and professionals is taught to seek immediate gratification in life, instead of perennial moral and ethical norms that will ensure long-term success and happiness.

The third source of statistical data concerns precisely the moral and ethical values. The political and corporate arena offers plenty of examples of professionals who ignore some of the most basic moral and ethical human values (telling the truth comes to mind). The results of many polls show where the level of values stands when it comes to sensitive questions on morality among voters (that level is very low). This is a telling example of one major result of an incomplete education, or rather of an education completed within an inefficient paradigm, the paradigm of separation. Even though many public figures claim strong ties with different religious denominations, it is evident that such affiliations have not been sufficiently convincing to avoid unlawful or immoral acts. The new educational paradigm of union I am proposing here, will set much more dependable norms. This can have tremendous implication on the political arena as well, which, in our democracy will affect many other major and vital components of modern life.

I am aware of the fact that it is a challenge to design and implement a procedure that instantaneously solves all problems, especially considering the human reluctance to change. However, I believe that people *can* change, especially when they are provided with solid reasons and clear benefits. As individuals, by realizing that in fact "we are all one," people will grow to respect each other and to treasure the environment since everything is part of the universal union.

The Concern

The main purpose of education is to provide personal and professional preparation in order to become a functional human being in the society. It is also evident that, even if we focus only on the most recent centuries, education did not eliminate, or did not even diminish the destructive aspect of human personal and social behavior. I think, therefore, that we should hold modern education to a much higher standard and responsibility.

A complete and accomplished educational system with high expectations for the future, should provide not only means of survival, but should also drastically reduce and eventually eliminate crime. Today's education performs very poorly at this task. The crime rate is high, which underlines that the old educational paradigm is inefficient. Most academic institutions function well in preparing students to become professionals, but when it comes to the moral education and the character of their graduates, we cannot be as impressed. As an educator I can say that we teach the necessary knowledge for the respective degree plan, but we leave the deeper moral, ethical, and spiritual development aside, probably assuming that somehow it will be reached on the job or in the family, community, and/or a variety of religious institutions. This fact contributes directly to the existence of the problem mentioned before: within a model of separation from everybody else and from nature, unaware of a possible deeper meaning of their lives, individuals perpetuate criminal tendencies within an apparent existential struggle. Consequently, crime is on the rise in the world, threatening real positive and long-lasting future progress.

With such an important concern in mind, we need to bring into the spot-light a major component of modern life, namely religion. In recent centuries education has been practiced hand in hand with religion, often the school being the church and the teacher being the priest or the minister. Therefore, it is logical to conclude that the contents of education and its presentation to students have been deeply influenced by their respective religious belief. Even today in the United States where institutionalized academic education is largely secular, the methodology, pedagogy, and general educational philosophy are still drastically influenced by the Christian doctrine. If we also consider the numerous private institutions that are affiliated directly with particular religious denominations, we can see that this influence is quite pervasive.

Such implications are definitely sensitive and become visible especially when a large part of the population is publicly involved, as for example within the perennial dispute around the issue of prayer in schools. This is a clear example of how previously educated generations affect the course of modern teaching and learning. When one considers education from the broader perspective as mentioned before, parents, friends, relatives, mass media, and even strangers, all have a direct impact also in how general religious beliefs are conveyed to today's youth in a non-academic educational context. Even within such a complex educational environment, which may include religious instruction, the problem persists. It seems that modern society, in spite of its unprecedented technological and educational advances, cannot successfully eliminate, or even substantially diminish general crime. Moreover, numerous recent events in our society show that the spirituality taught in most Christian environments does not "bless" people with the necessary common sense and self determined incentive in order to eliminate crime and self destructive behavior. Even worse, often clerics themselves trespass the moral and ethical Christian code. For example, as recent developments show, some Catholic priests have been disciplined for sexual misconduct.

Consequently, there is an imperative need for a shift in the present paradigm in order for education to achieve its goal of creating dependable and responsible professionals. In addition, general education should help people become sensitive human beings, ready to embrace a truly evolved future.

The Purpose of this Book

The first decade of a millennium is such a unique moment in time that we should reflect intensely on the real meaning of human existence and, as a result, on what we can do to improve the quality of life on Earth. Since education has a definite impact on our future, and since we are getting our education through such a large variety of means, I think it is tremendously important to do whatever it takes to change the negative human trends into positive ones. It is my conviction that the message of this book and its implementation will yield extraordinary outcomes.

Education within a technological society cannot aspire to greatness unless it provides a logical, common sense explanation of the deeper meaning of what is being studied, including the meaning of human life. Today, with a limited, although practical sense in mind, the educator generally presents knowledge intended to ensure tomorrow's successful "producer" in whatever line of work. Seldom is the larger picture of the meaning of that work presented, let alone its philosophical implication for humanity. Furthermore, most classroom focus, from grade school through college, for the most part excludes preparation having to do with the purpose of human life on Earth, and the impact each person has in the world. Such a limited education deprives the student of a key self motivator: the realization that we are all one. The purpose of this book is to show that we all are indispensable parts of a larger whole, interdependent, and interconnected. Once we become aware of this reality, we will effortlessly involve ourselves in positive and constructive actions in our lives, realizing that the opposite practice is self destructive.

Positive and constructive teaching is generally the intention of educators, especially parents. However, regardless of how well intended we are, we cannot effectively teach what we don't know and understand ourselves. Therefore, another important purpose of this book is to show how we all can assimilate the needed knowledge that, when taught to others, can really make a difference in the world. The new paradigm of union presents exactly the core components of such a system of knowledge. Once the educational chain that includes complete and effective common sense teaching is put in place, the positive outcomes will be impressive. The level of personal responsibility will rise, the crime rate will decrease, and a sense of unity within our society will prevail.

Union Versus Separation

Modern life can be described by some of the most important human endeavors, which offers an opportunity to analyze closely social trends, both positive and negative. My focus is on religion, science, and the recent explosion in the high-tech field, as well as on modern education in the West.

The Christian religion in general teaches a doctrine of triple separation: humans are separated from God, God is separated from nature, and we are to fight nature under a presumed divine order to dominate it. Even more, human beings are taught that they are separated from each other, which creates, especially in a heterogeneous society, racial and gender problems of a large magnitude.

Over the centuries, this separation doctrine has infiltrated the entire education system. As a consequence, people possess a clear picture of this separation in full accordance with the old paradigm religiously maintained. It is no surprise that the level of personal responsibility stays low, and immoral and unethical ways of living are wide-spread. In this book I propose that general education can benefit us all through the change of the existing paradigm of separation into one of union.

In contrast to the classic Christian view, there is another picture of the universe offered by religions and spiritual traditions of the East. Centuries before Christ, Hinduism and Buddhism, to mention only two, had presented a picture of inclusion and union of all that is. With this in mind, I propose the possibility of adopting such a philosophy for modern education. Fortunately, the 20th century provided science with some of the most revolutionary discoveries in history. My focus is on one in particular, namely quantum mechanics or quantum physics. This book includes testimonies given over the years by well known researchers in this impressive field. Quantum mechanics supports the aforementioned Eastern philosophical views, thereby finally connecting science with spirituality. Furthermore, the theory of morphic resonance and morphic fields, the research area of the prominent contemporary biologist Rupert Sheldrake, is attracting more attention lately. This theory, based on the results of many well documented experiments, sets forth a relatively new support for the universal union paradigm.

Another subject of investigation that has important implications in education, religion, and science is the difference in meaning between the term *religion* and that of *spirituality*. This distinction is rarely acknowledged by religious exponents, but nevertheless is present in many schools of thought. It is becoming a significant way of presenting the differences between the doctrine of separation and that of universal union or the concept of quantum interconnection.

Chapter 2:

What Really Matters

---

*In each action we must look beyond the action at our
past,
present, and future state, and at others whom it affects,
and see the relation of all those things.
And then we shall be very cautious.*

Blaise Pascal

Human Existence

Teaching and learning is taking place on many planes of human existence, which is why I approach the core subject of this book from different perspectives. I believe that all experiences we have are equally important in shaping our characters, especially in determining moral and ethical values. The importance of a good character is easily understood: one quick look at our past is sufficient to motivate us to do better in regard to our children's education as far as character building is concerned.

We in the Western world should embrace a set of fundamental perennial human values as part of the patrimony of any respectful society. But statistics display a clear picture of an undesirable state of affairs in this respect.

The most impressive advances of the human race are both positive and negative, raising the question: Is there a constructive planetary future if we base our development on such fragile foundations? Directing general education mainly toward the material side of life appears to be one of the most detrimental long-term human endeavors, and the results of this orientation are already evident.

This is true not only within the laic part of our society, but also deep in the Christian clergy. Understanding the origin of Christianity, the origin of the Bible, and the Christian influence in modern Western education will help us understand our current condition. This includes academic settings, as well as education acquired in the family, among friends, and through involvement and participation in church, sports, and society at large.

There is abundant information available on education toward a new set of fundamental values in religion, spirituality, self growth, self-improvement, and sciences. All of this is meant to unite humans, nature, and God, as opposed to the existing philosophy of separation. A large volume of well documented works which point toward the need for a new language in education shows that the present secular aspect of Western life is slowly giving room to a more sacred way of living.

The Western way of life requires scientific proof for any new theory put forth. However, as religious and/or spiritual matters are concerned, this is not always possible; many well known scientists released their professional scrutiny and explored spiritual areas with instinctive devotion and conviction. Some of the greatest pioneers in physics, biology, and space travel speak from their common sense based on many decades of analytical work, and they present a surprising new and different picture of the universe. To these scientists the spiritual realm is not as foreign as some might expect. However, as always, there will be those who find the spiritual exploration meaningless, which offers an interesting debate.

Designing a new paradigm for more efficient education is possible. I believe that understanding the sensitive traits of the new model that includes essential elements of union versus the separation paradigm is the way to better living.

The Origin of the Separation Paradigm

The history of Western culture shows very interesting developments over the centuries, an evolution that can be surprising to the scientifically oriented eye. One culmination on the scientific realm is the discipline of Physics. The term itself is derived from the Greek word *physis*, which stands for the essential nature of things. It was used in the sixth century B.C. by the Milesian school from Ionia, in an attempt to discover the real constitution of the material world[1]. Since the Milesians did not differentiate between animate and inanimate objects, their philosophy is similar to that of the Eastern spirituality of India and China. Even closer parallels may be found in the philosophy of Heraclitus of Ephesus, who supported the view of a world in eternal becoming. He maintained that the changes we witness around us are caused by the interplay of pairs of opposites. Each pair of opposites was understood as a solid unity called Logos which is beyond the forces involved in the play.

This unity awareness was not to last very long because the Eleatic school slowly removed from the world the assumed implicit Divine Principle that was directing it, placing it somewhere outside the world. Such was the beginning of the separation of matter and spirit, the well known dualism in Western philosophy.

As a continuation of this process, Parmenides of Elea offered a philosophy opposing even more strongly that of Heraclitus. Greek philosophers of the fifth century B.C. attempted to soften the contrasts of the two views. Therefore, they proposed that the unchangeable Being of Parmenides manifests itself in some invariable substances, giving birth to the idea of the atom. Starting with Leucippus and Democritus, the Greek atomists suggested that matter is made of some building blocks, clearly separating matter and spirit. They explained the movement and the energy of matter as being caused by external forces of spiritual origin, which are different than matter itself. Thus the distinction between mind and matter and between body and soul took its solid place in the Western philosophical tradition.

This kind of thought was later adopted by Aristotle, whose teachings served as the basis of Western philosophy for many centuries to come. Even so, Aristotle was inclined to think that questions regarding the nature of the human soul and the perfection of God are more important than the study of matter. With the support of the Christian Church and with so little interest in the study of the material world, Aristotle's philosophical scheme remained unchallenged for a long time.

The end of the Middle Ages marked a change in Western thought and during the Renaissance many thinkers began complementing and eventually overtaking the influence of the Church and the Aristotelian model. Galileo became the founder of science as we know it by introducing mathematics in combination with empirical knowledge. Still, Descartes separated mind and matter into two different areas, thereby opening the door for scientists to treat matter as an entity existing outside of themselves. The universe appears now as a machine and within this understanding the physics of Isaac Newton led the scientific world view until the end of the 19th century. Within this picture:

> The fundamental laws of nature searched for by the scientists were thus seen as laws of God, invariable and eternal, to which the world was subjected.[2]

It is important to realize that, beside directing classical physics, the philosophy of Descartes also inclined most Westerners to see themselves as individual and separated egos who live in their physical bodies. Consequently, there seemed to be a conflict between the involuntary instincts and the free will. Even more, this belief created the frustration of human beings as they think they live within separate material cells determined by individual feelings, talents, wishes, etc. Lifelong attempts to become better, richer, faster, or smarter than others, have set people on a path of competition within separation, causing most of the well-known turmoil in the world. The belief in such separation not only manifests itself at the personal level, but also drastically affects relationships between families, social, political, and religious groups, and culminates with international disagreement and war.

Although the Cartesian separation paradigm favored the development of science and technology as we know it in the West, it also caused many negative effects. One area of paramount importance affected by the doctrine of separation is the set of real values people implement in their lives.

Life's Real Values

Moral and ethical norms are determined and set in place by the general popular philosophical convictions of the society. Such convictions spring from the level of individual acceptance of the respective philosophical concepts. The social group that helps materialize this acceptance is composed of all active providers of education. In this respect, families, schools, churches, places of employment, and entertainment establishments join in shaping the essential set of practical moral and ethical values of the individual.

However, none of the aforementioned educational providers can "teach" values which are not *already* part of their present existential philosophy; or in other words, one cannot teach something one does not know. Therefore, we can clearly see that within a scientific picture of separation between the material and the spiritual makeup of the universe, the values that will be promoted will follow suit. That is why we witness today in the Western world the manifestation of a set of values that mirror this separation philosophy within every area of human endeavor. The ego drives people to selfish acts of survival (most like in the animal kingdom) based on an existential philosophy that maintains the idea of separation from God (or the spiritual universe) and also separation from nature.

This separation is indeed an illusion caused by the limited perception human beings experience through the five senses. But, for the time being, let us examine which moral and ethical values should really matter.

It is evident that the human race has been searching for such traits regardless of the historical and geographical scene. All religions and mythological traditions show a path of discovery, testing and implementing moral and ethical standards. From time to time, whenever a logical and common sense understanding of a norm is missing, strict laws are passed in order to impose social acceptance and compliance. These kinds of values, in need of such regulation and being frequently trespassed, show the fruit of the scientific and religious doctrine of separation.

Here is one simple example. Many people are convinced that, under special circumstances, it is okay to lie. Upon further inspection, we realize that telling the truth is the one most frequently broken law from the well known Ten Commandments of Christianity, for example. In all walks of life, from small and seemingly unimportant personal situations to international political intrigues, people hide the truth. Even under oath some individuals think that their cause is more important than telling the truth (one can find many examples from the political arena and the corporate world). Why? Why do people think that if they are not caught telling a lie, everything is well? The answer to this question is given by the kind of education these individuals received. From families, relatives, and friends, to churches, academic institutions, and the military, the message put forth by living examples of high moral and ethical

standards is not convincing people that they *must*, under any circumstance tell the truth. Instead, they find excuses to justify their
lies. We can, therefore, see that the truthfulness is one important
brick in the solid wall of the new paradigm of union. Within a
model of complete interconnection I maintain that one must tell the
truth at all times and in all situations especially with the understanding that lying to others is not only undermining one self's
credibility but also is creating negative self repercussions in the
future. After all, would we, *ourselves*, like to be lied to?

I would like to focus now on the nature of real values that
should guide our lives. What we should consider real norms are
those that build an unshakable human character throughout one's
life. Real values must be those which are effective regardless of
ones material possessions, age, nationality, gender, religious
belief, or political orientation. Real values are those that do not
fluctuate according to our immediate interests. Real values should
keep people happy, together, within an atmosphere of healthy and
constructive interpersonal relationships. They should manifest
within families, within groups of friends sharing interests, within
religious and political configurations, within any kind of professional establishment, and should be an integral part of random
interaction between total strangers. Real values should be timeless
and unconditional, leading to positiveness, peace, and hope for a
better world.

Besides truthfulness, the value that impacts our lives the most
is love. As we examine different areas of human existence, we
notice that wherever love is present, people stay together, live in
harmony, work much more productively than otherwise, and interact in positive and efficient ways with each other. It is not an accident that most marriages are based on love, which clearly reflects
that love unites, while its opposite, or the lack of, separates and
estranges people. Another obvious example of the manifestation of
love is the instinctive affection of parents for their children. It is
this kind of love that keeps families together, united within the
supreme goal of mutual happiness.

In the Western world, where the material side of life is so
important, love often appears as a norm conditioned by outcomes
of events external to the direct human interaction. Many pretend to
love others *if*, and then they list conditions. Many loving relation-

ships start with promises of forever, but after a while something happens and that love cannot be preserved without some fulfilled conditions. Why? Why do people change their perception of love so often and so drastically? The answer is in the fact that many people do not know who they really are and have been educated within a philosophy of separation.

Here is a list of other high standard human traits that we should all cherish: patience, understanding the needs of others, humility, affection, compassion, charity, modesty, and forgiveness. One of these traits, charity, is presented in the Bible by the Apostle Paul as love or the equivalent of love:

1 Though I speak with the tongues of men and of angels, and have not charity, I am become as sounding brass, or a tinkling symbol.
2 And though I have the gift of prophesy, and understand all mysteries, and all knowledge; and though I have all faith, so I could remove mountains, and have not charity, I am nothing.
3 And though I bestow all my goods to feed the poor, and though I give my body to be burned, and have not charity, it profiteth me nothing.
4 Charity suffereth long, and is kind; charity envieth not; charity vaunteth not itself, is not puffed up,
5 Doth not behave itself unseemly, seeketh not her own, is not easily provoked, thinketh no evil;
6 Rejoyceth not in iniquity, but rejoyceth in the truth;
7 Beareth all things, believeth all things, hopeth all things, endureth all things[3].

Indeed, unconditional love as charity should transcend all aspects of the material world that stand in the way of its purity. We witness here an understanding of love and compassion as manifestations of the spiritual side of human existence. However, the doctrine of separation, which is the existing paradigm, makes the practical implementation of such a high standard of human behavior difficult. People, more often than not, admire and recognize high norms, but find it hard to effectively assimilate them in their everyday life. Consequently, the opposites of the desirable human values prevail in many cultural environments, from the personal, which might appear insignificant, to families, communities, and finally, to all of society.

As exemplified in the previous chapter, it is evident that over the last few decades, although our society made obvious technological and economic progress, the implementation of higher moral and ethical values has stagnated, at best. It seems that many people have been neglecting exactly those values which make them human. It also appears that the general pursuit of a higher material living standard has blinded many, causing their ethical and moral values not to improve and in many cases to slip to lower levels.

Why do people behave in such unacceptable fashion? I think the answer is inevitable: The present view of the world, the educational paradigm of separation is not effective enough to convince all of us of the paramount importance of proper behavior. Even more, in spite of the unprecedented technological and economical development, meaningful education has been left behind. By this I don't mean that technology and financial resources have not been made available in modern education; indeed they are available. Rather, education has not evolved into a more efficient human endeavor, capable of explaining the place we really occupy in the universe. The technological explosion of the last 30 years and new trends in modern education have greatly impacted teaching and learning in the new Millennium.

Within a society ruled by technology, striving exclusively for material gain results in neglecting some of the most common-sense ethical and moral norms of behavior. Consequently, statistics show how the rise in crime and violence implied a rise in the number of law enforcement professionals. For example, from 1960 to 1991 there was an increase in the number of Supreme Court lawyers from 285,933 to 805,872 respectively.

The alarming statistics on crime and violence imply also the tip of another iceberg: that of the national expense required in order to treat such a state of affairs. Who is actually paying for all the unsuccessful attempts to address the problem? The next common sense question should be: If the crime rate were much lower (ideally nonexistent), what constructive and progressive human endeavors could benefit from the extra financial resources available? Here are some examples: poor public school districts, higher education, health education, treatment of presently incurable illnesses such as cancer and AIDS, pollution, agriculture, hunger, and so on. It is obvious that if we can make available a better way to eliminate or at least to drastically diminish criminal behavior, all of the present resources devoted to remedying it could be redirected. As important an issue as crime is, we must not forget other crucial areas of interest for the human race, such as the environment. Modern society seems to neglect the very source of its existence: the natural habitat.

The solution we are seeking should be incorporated in the modern education under the new paradigm of union. This could be the real treatment for any type of crime and environmental abuse; even better, *real* education, the common sense education that explains the *reasons* for certain social and existential ethical and moral values, will actually *prevent* detrimental activities from happening in the first place, just as preventive care is encouraged in medicine. However, people need to be presented with logical evidence in order to incorporate the components of such a "preventive" attitude. This is exactly the core of the new educational paradigm I propose as a model of logical thinking that applies to all walks of life. When everybody is aware that *we are all one*, united at a much grander level than we have been taught, people would not strike at others. Convinced of this reality parents will be able to teach it to their children from day one, educational institutions will widely incorporate it in their curriculum, and, once generalized, people will live as one in all their interactions.

As a contrast to such a positive picture, the present model of separation suggests a dim future. Statistics, paired with our firsthand experience, show no improvement in the crime rate over the last decades. Therefore, most of the educational efforts, though positively intended, have been essentially wasted. There must be a better way.

Chapter 3:

Electrifying Experiences

God never wrought miracle to convince atheism,
because his ordinary works convince it.

Francis Bacon

Implications of Technology

Over the ages human efforts have been mainly channeled toward making life easier, healthier, and more pleasant. Within this context, technological innovations have been made in order to reduce the brute force required to survive, to improve health, and to offer people a chance to enjoy their free time. However positive this intent may be, each innovation also carries risks and possible destructive implications.

The discovery that facilitated the avalanche of all the other 20th century technological marvels has been the electric current, and today we are dependent on it. The most essential tools, machinery, appliances, computers, telephones, stereos, and even toys function on electricity. The second half of the 20th century has been marked by impressive advances in electronics. The later decades of the last century witnessed the infiltration of computer technology into virtually every major area of modern life. From food preparation to entertainment, to educational software and satellites, computer technology has become indispensable. The manufacture and distribution of computer technology have become the fastest growing business opportunities of our time.

As computer availability increased tremendously, people began to appreciate the new technology especially for the speed of execution of preprogrammed tasks, for the capability of storing vast amounts of information, and for the world wide access to such information. The initial use of networked computers was in the United States military. As time passed, this use was expended into other areas, and today millions benefit from the opportunity to communicate with people all over the world by means of electronic mail. Due to the impressive storage capacity, electronic data banks make entire libraries available globally to business owners and interested researchers. Also the latest news is instantly available by a click of a computer mouse.

With all these facilities at our fingertips, it was only natural to employ computers in the realm of education. From their use in reading, writing, science, and mathematics classrooms, to "distance learning," computers have become an integral part of modern teaching and learning. However, a closer look at their role in some educational areas shows that this technology is in fact only a mechanical intermediary between teacher and student. In an era when real human values seem to be more and more neglected, it is obvious that employing an insensitive, electronic connection at the crossroads of teaching and learning might not always be a good idea. In his *Data Smog: Surviving the Information Glut*, David Shenk says it clearly under "The Laws of Data Smog": "Computers are neither human nor humane" and "Putting a computer in every classroom is like putting an electric power plant in every home." Indeed, the classroom was primarily designed as a conveyer of *selected* knowledge, not as a facilitator of a flood of information.

Although for some people's personality a computerized intermediary might be recommended, from a psychological point of view it only serves to separate, or alienate, and to diminish the eye to eye human contact. The picture of a teaching computer lab often shows isolated individuals in front of insensitive machines. Some educators propose a departure from the classical "classroom lecture" style of teaching, favoring "computer mediated" teaching or even more, "distance learning." As we look closer at this picture we should ask some questions. First, within the computer mediated learning isn't it the computer actually lecturing to the student? Second, as a consequence, which kind of lecture should we prefer: a preprogrammed insensitive computer lecture or that from a sensitive human being as the instructor in the classroom?

Moreover, the extensive implementation of "cutting-edge" technology may appear to unite people by offering super fast means of communication. In fact, the opposite may be true. Under the illusion of talking to, or even seeing the other person on a screen, we are kept *physically* apart. The much praised accomplishment of virtual reality should be an important warning sign for the loss of appreciation of true *reality* as the world presents it to us. To experience a mountain climb while you are wired up on a seat in some movie theater, regardless of the felt authenticity of the electronically induced event, cannot substitute the real experience of being on your own feet, smelling the unique alpine aromas in the pure air, as you feel your heartbeat propelling you through the grand scenery.

Therefore, we can already identify three major side effects to high-technology: (1) overwhelming and tempting availability of information, which for many is really not necessary, (2) physical separation between people, and (3) alienation from the true and wonderful natural realities of our world. The latter of the three raises another point of concern. Since new forms of high-tech entertainment have the capacity to create virtual excitement with little or no effort, more and more people are embracing such entertainment. Modern technology brings super realistic scenes to our eyes, ears, and minds either on the large cinema screen, computers or on the home television set. Violence in the news and in the entertainment realm has been condemned by many social and religious groups as detrimental to young and old. If we keep in mind the natural human inclination to experience excitement, we understand how high-tech creation of virtual realities can instigate the exploration of new possibilities for real, but often dangerous endeavors. From the sad reality of drug abuse and the danger of "extreme" sports (sky-diving, bunjie jumping, extreme skateboarding, etc.), to the technologically induced fear on occasions such as the extreme celebration of Halloween, recent years show a general tendency to push even the "fun" we desire to unsafe and often deadly levels.

Although there are many positive implications of high-technology, it can also be said that it facilitates manifestation of immoral behavior. In this respect the Internet opens up avenues for those inclined to pornography and pedophilia. In recent years, loss of privacy and stolen identities were also at the top of the list of negative use of technology. The FBI files speak volumes to this kind of abuse. More so, as we remember 9/11 and many other anti human acts, we should take notice of the use of high-tech in terrorist activities around the world.

Let us next consider the effects of the high processing speed

offered by most electronic gadgets. In terms of obtaining information in a timely manner, such speed is to be appreciated; however,
in many other areas of life it can have long-term detrimental
effects. One negative long-term effect concerns our own health.
From children to adults, as we compare today's life to that of some
decades ago, we tend to rush more and more in everything we do.
Whether going to school, or attending a soccer practice, or going to
the movies, from a young age many of us live with the eyes on the
clock. Educational institutions and practically every other source
of teaching and learning seems to preach the same lesson: faster is
better. Since "faster" seemingly saves time, we obviously ignore
the quality of the experience for the sake of more experiential volume squeezed into the same 24-hour day. We see long lines of cars
around unhealthy fast-food restaurants, we see people having
breakfast or getting ready for work while driving, we see ourselves
eating lunch while working, and then, by not paying attention to all
of these realities, we act surprised by the high rate of heart problems, obesity, anxieties, and other long-term negative consequences.

One of the greatest human virtues that we sacrifice in our pursuit of this fast paced lifestyle is *patience*. As we strive to *do* and *be*
more on our jobs, or at home, we loose patience. We don't have the
time to patiently talk to a coworker, a friend, or even a member of
our own family. We justify such behavior by pretending that being
involved in more activities is really more important than building
positive and sensitive human relationships. What is even worse is
that, as adults, deeply submerged in this lifestyle, we actually teach
it to our youth by example. We seem to forget the well known saying "the best thing you can give to your children is your time."

Saving time (and of course making money) has been the main
motivation behind the mass production of a large variety of fancy
electronic (often programmable) appliances, and we all know the
multitude of time-saving gadgets present in modern homes. But the
obvious question arises: what ever happened to the large amount of
time saved by employing them? Indeed, it seems that we have less
and less time for ourselves and our immediate families than our
parents or grandparents had. Regarding the actual time spent working, it is worth noting that in some societies people used to have

more holidays than working days in a year. As the world "evolves," the amount of time for celebration, rest, and appreciation of life is substantially decreased. This reality not only determines our actual vision of the world, but also dictates the way we understand our personal life.

After all these considerations we can see how a change in our existential paradigm is necessary in order to create a better future. Most of the trends discussed earlier spring from the separation model we live in today. The union paradigm I am proposing is meant to liberate us from modern addictions, and through a deeper understanding of who we are and what we are here for, to allow us to use safely and efficiently all the technological advances we treasure.

Real Goals of Education

Especially in the West, the materialistic mentality contributes to a one-sided human development. Absorbed in the struggle for survival or material prosperity, we channel our energy into an area determined by the separation model sustained by Newtonian Physics. Within the image of a mechanical universe we see ourselves caught in a physical drama, where good luck, bad luck, winning, losing, victims, and accidents are understood as an implicit and natural part of the play. The use of questions such as "What?" and "How?" out-number by far the deeper and more meaningful inquiry expressed by the question "Why?" It is definitely more important to have a reason for what we think, say, or do, instead of only asking "what" and "how" in order to do them. Such a practice will be vital within the new paradigm of union, where any part of the whole knows intrinsically the answer to the question "why?"

My own experience in the field of education has taught me that most standard teaching methodologies are focused on student's learning the mechanical steps to solve a problem, at the expense of thoroughly understanding the *reasons* behind the respective steps. As an example, profit oriented educational private companies launched powerful campaigns to replace rigorous academic teaching of mathematics in the classroom, by "teaching to the test" strategies. This provided short term results (better scores on standardized tests), which made them famous over the years. However, a close examination of their curriculum and methodology, reveals that such teaching is a *mechanical* educational endeavor at best; students are rarely confronted with the question "why?" a certain procedure works. This approach deprives students of deeper and more meaningful learning and produces a shallow long-term education.

Not only is this attempt purely business oriented, but it is also a perfect example of modern educational efforts within the old materialistic model meant to reach immediate goals regardless of the long-term implications. By excluding almost completely the focus on "Why?"—which, by the way, is the question children ask most in their attempt to understand the world—long-term negative patterns are put in place. Consequently, we notice a general attitude of often senseless competition, which reminds us of the survival struggle in the animal kingdom. Very seldom do questions like why, why are we here, who are we, where are we heading, what happens after death, and what is our real place in the universe come to people's minds.

We must recognize that the old educational paradigm of separation only rarely raises such questions; the importance of many real human values is minimized or completely neglected. On April 13, 1997, David Wallechinsky published in *Parade Magazine* the results of an international survey in an article entitled "Are We Still Number One?" The article begins thus:

> Ten years ago, PARADE reported on the categories in which our country [the United States] led the world, as well as those in which we trailed other nations. Many things have changed in the last decade—both at home and abroad. There are new technologies and new health problems, not to mention new fads and new tastes. Where have we improved from our earlier position, and where have we fallen behind?

The article states that in 1986, although "we were neck-and-neck with the Soviet Union in military power and way ahead in economic power," the United States fell behind many nations in terms of health, education, and prevention of crime. As of 1996 the United States is number one in Nobel Prize-winners, computers used at home, gross national product, campers, production of paper, plastics, and cigarettes, foreign university students, and populations of Christians and Jews. We are *not* number one in number of daily newspapers, minimal fat consumption, movie theaters, number of rooms per living unit, geothermal energy, minimal divorce rate, and life expectancy for men and women. During the decade in question, the divorce rate jumped from fourth to second place, ranking the United States right behind the Maldives[5], while in the number of published book titles the United States ranks fifth, compared to being number one a decade earlier. As education is concerned, the study shows that "American primary and secondary school students rank quite far from No. 1, particularly in math, science and geography."

The article continues to list rankings in other vital areas of life. Crime in our country is still embarrassing in the eyes of the civilized world:

> According to the most recent Interpol figures, the United States has the 23rd highest murder rate among 95 nations (the second highest among industrialized nations, after Russia), the seventh highest rape rate, 11th highest serious assault rate and the third highest violent theft rate.

Although health expense per capita has risen, the decade from 1986 to 1996 shows a drop in almost all categories of health care. In 1986 the United States was number 12 in infant mortality, while in 1996 there were 28 nations with lower infant mortality rates.

The article ends with a quote from educator and author Jonathan Kozol:

> We are the most powerful, the toughest and the richest. But we could also be the most benign and the most decent nation. We are capable of being great and good at the same time.

More recently, the January 14, 2007 edition of the same magazine presents an update on the place United States of America holds in the world in some crucial social areas. Here is where we are No. 1: billionaires, 2004 Olympic medals, Internet users, Nobel

Prize-winners, military abroad, miles of roads, airports, and gold reserves. However, the article concludes:

> America needs to do better in some critical areas: Doctors—43 countries have more physicians per capita than we do, Infant deaths—33 countries have lower rates, Male life expectancy—residents of 27 countries live longer, Murders—15th-highest murder rate, Prisons— highest per capita rate of people in prison, Women in national legislatures—71 countries do better, Voting—of eligible citizens who vote, U.S. is 139th of 172 nations."

Sources of Information

In order to be "great and good at the same time" we need to reevaluate our national priorities, namely those concerning the general education. As more evidence to the shortcomings of the present educational paradigm is made available, the need for a new, more efficient model becomes more pressing. Since education takes place in such a wide variety of ways besides just the institutionalized academic channels, let us examine some other important sources of information and their messages.

It is safe to say that the almost universal avenue for general information to reach modern American households is the television program. Although there are some people who don't own a TV set, an overwhelming number do. Considering the fact that in many homes there are more than one set, and that most people watch several hours of television per day, we can also understand why this medium of claimed entertainment acts very powerfully as an educational tool. Going beyond the daily hours of sitcoms, dramas, movies, and sporting events, a large variety of programming available today offers real educational experiences for young and old. From Disney and Nickelodeon, to Discovery and The Learning Channel, informative programs enhance our personal bank of information. If we also consider weekly network news programs such as *20/20*, *60 Minutes*, *Date Line*, *Night Line*, *48 Hours*, and

Prime Time Live we realize how vast are the educational opportunities by means of television.

Most of these educational programs present information meant to amend the quality of our lives, and often they contain vital warnings concerning the present and the future of our society. From updates on healthcare issues, to coverage of global warming and the dangers of international nuclear proliferation, well documented programs appeal to a wide variety of viewers. That is why the knowledge we acquire by means of television plays a very important role in the general education.

However, regardless of how convincing these programs are, in order to effectively implement their positive teaching in our lives, we need more of a hands-on experience. As a clear example, I would like to comment on two impressive studies presented on The Learning Channel, entitled *Cyber Warriors* and *Future War*. They describe the downside of the information explosion we are witnessing in the West through the creation of the Internet. It is evident that as the state of the art computer technology is available worldwide, it is available to "everybody" who has the financial capability to purchase it. Therefore, the same technology used in positive and constructive human endeavors may also be used by those with anti human goals. Top military secrets have been stolen, entire data libraries have been lost, and misinformation has been disseminated via the Internet. The fact is that all of this has been made possible with the same electronic tools that others hope to use to find solutions to humankind's problems. The ease of almost instant communication between people facilitates crime, as does the electronic availability of information. This kind of reality is not hard to understand in a society where most entrepreneurs will do anything to boost their profits. Business on the Web is so popular because of the ease of operating in cyberspace. People are able to conduct business from their homes, very often with no physical contact with others. Gambling, "Cyber Casino," is one of the latest fastest growing international business on the Internet. Advertised as gaming, much of the activity is illegal.

And that is the trap: within a mind-set of separation and individual success, we forget that, in fact, we all depend on each other. Business on the Internet, communication via an electronic screen (even when the other person lives next door), and distance learning, are all alternatives to more traditional human activities, but we must not lose sight of the fact that we are still *human beings*. What makes us unique in the entire animal kingdom on Earth, are the emotional traits that allow us to cry, to laugh, to show love and compassion, to mourn, to invent, to create, to forgive, and to pray.

All these sensitive human characteristics can be preserved and enhanced, so long as we remain aware of their importance in our lives. This kind of awareness comes through day-by-day education. There are so many examples all around us where, in the name of better, faster, and more profitable, we destroy the natural habitat, only to be forced to come back later to fix it, most often at great expense. Prevention is the best cure. Many of the national and worldwide catastrophes caused by the human race in recent times are the result of misusing our most sophisticated technological creations.

As a consequence, by following blindly the educational model of the past we cannot avoid repeating the same mistakes. Education is not only the source to common sense understanding of existing problems, but it is also the road to finding long-lasting solutions. The new paradigm of union provides solid reasoning in order to help us motivate ourselves in the process of finding such solutions.

Chapter 4:

Religious Influence on Modern Times

Religion without science is blind.
Science without religion is lame.

Albert Einstein

An Overview of Biblical Writings

Ever since the birth of the United States of America, institutional-ized education has been evolving hand in hand with the dominant Christian religion introduced by the first pilgrims. Following faith-fully the European model of integrating teaching, learning, and religious practice, an educational system based on biblical doctrine was put in place. In the beginning, the minister was also the teacher. Later, well defined and specialized professional careers became the norm in education. As new demands arose, more teach-ers embraced languages, arts, sciences, physical education, and sports, creating over the years a diversified school system. Although the variety of curriculum presently implemented in decentralized school districts around the country is truly impres-sive, we must recognize that the basic teaching philosophy shared across disciplines is consistent with the later Greek model of sep-aration: the paradigm that considers humans physically separated from nature and from God.

It is very interesting to notice that the Greek philosophical view of the separation of material and spiritual existence was refined during the fifth and fourth centuries B.C., which means that at the time of Christ, this way of thinking had been in place in the Hellenic world for at least 400 years. Since the Roman Empire occupied such a vast territory, the core of the Greek philosophy spread with time, thereby making its way also into the geographi-cal region in which the biblical events took place.

From the inception of Christianity, to its institutionalization as a stand-alone religion, away from its Jewish roots, three centuries had to pass. In the first quarter of the fourth century A.D., Emperor Constantine the Great, with the idea of creating a powerful religion to sustain the Roman Empire, ordered the First Council of Nicea to convene. The council met in 325 A.D. with the charge to select the authentic sacred Christian writings from those of other origins, and to compile them in one single book. Approximately 300 church-men of various religious backgrounds convened in the midst of dissension, jealousy, intolerance, and persecution to accomplish this important task. Constantine called himself a Christian and imposed the newly created doctrine throughout his empire.

The ambiance in which the "book of books," or the Bible, was originally assembled suggests some possible inconsistencies, and later turns of events created even more suspicion about its contents. We need to remember that the first books of the New Testament were written originally in Greek, while the actual language in which the presumed events took place was Aramaic. Moreover, the earliest book was committed to writing at least 30 years after the actual events related to the life and death of Jesus, a fact that can be used to question the accuracy of its contents. Hundreds of years later, in 533 A.D., at the Second Council of Constantinople, Emperor Justinian ordered a revision of the biblical writings. At this council a strange decree was adopted: "Whosoever shall support the mythical doctrine of the preexistence of the soul and the subsequent wonderful opinion of its return, let him be anathema."6 Since one cannot cancel something nonexistent, this decree alone proves that the 200-year old book contained some teachings (in this case the idea of reincarnation) which were not pleasing to the people in power.7 Therefore, they used their authority to eliminate unwanted messages. Notable is the fact that the Pope boycotted the meeting, anticipating the mistreatment of the sacred writings that were at the foundation of the Catholic Church.

Based on these arguments, we can see how the biblical writings of the sixth century started to convey the picture of political dominance of the people in power. They continue to serve this purpose into the 21st century. Considering the 14-century history of the Bible since the Council of Constantinople, it is common sense to

assume that even more changes have been inflicted into the original content. In 2005, Professor Bart D. Ehrman, Chair of the
Department of Religious Studies at The University of North Carolina at Chapel Hill, put together a set of lectures on audio tape for
The Teaching Company entitled *The History of the Bible: The Making of the New Testament Canon.* Among the 12 lectures we find
some that are illustrative for the subject at hand. In lecture 4, entitled "The Problem of Pseudonymity," Professor Ehrman maintains
that some of the real authors of the writings of the New Testament
are not known. In this respect some writings have been attributed
to well known figures in order to make them more credible. In lecture 9, entitled "The Copyists Who Gave Us Scripture," he presents
the case of errors registered in the process of manual copying of the
scriptures. Professor Ehrman cites obvious discrepancies between
different manuscripts such as missing a word, an entire line, or
even an entire page. In lecture 10, "Authority in the Early Church"
and lecture 11, "The Importance of Interpretation" he focuses on
other obvious chances for changes over the centuries to the original meaning of the writings of the New Testament. One should also
consider the important case made about the many translations we
have today. It is well known that during a translation from one language to another there are sometimes severe cultural limitations in
the choice of words and even in the interpretation of the original
meaning.
    Another important fact is the actual time when translations of
the Bible in different languages took place. Here is a sample of
years and languages: 1466 German, 1471 Italian, 1526 Dutch,
1530 French, 1553 Spanish, 1685 Irish, 1688 Romanian, 1751 Por-
tuguese, 1871 Bulgarian, 1875 Russian, 1903 Ukrainian, 1990
Macedonian.[8] Whether we look forward or backward from the time
of the translation, we should ask how many people (human beings
with private interests) have had the opportunity to add, omit, or
simply change some of the contents of the Bible. Therefore, we
should not be surprised by the multiple discords born over centuries around different interpretations of the biblical writings.
    However, one such interpretation, and perhaps the most widely
spread in the West, is consistent with the separation model promoted by philosophers who subscribe to Aristotle's ideas. The
belief that humans are separated from God, and from nature, which

is also separated from God, builds a mechanistic model of the universe where God gives to humans free will and dominion over nature, but simultaneously, humans are to be sinful, weak, and not trustworthy. In turn, God governs the laws of the cosmos and rewards or punishes humans according to their deeds.

This is the picture presented to the faithful population by those who wanted the Bible to be their instrument of imposing fear, subordination to church and state power, and for financial gain. By institutionalizing heaven and hell, as actual places of reward and, respectively, eternal punishment, the fundamentalist Christian Church teaches moral and ethical values by force, simply warning humans that the only alternative is damnation. However, in spite of all the inevitable changes that took place over the centuries, a closer study of the biblical writings presents us with a much more complete picture, and reveals some interesting surprises.

Of course, in order to clearly understand the holistic meaning of these scriptures, one needs to take into consideration the time period in which they were put together. Historically, it is very well known that other religious and spiritual traditions had been in place long before the collection of the biblical texts. Such is the case of Hinduism, Buddhism, and other eastern philosophies. Here is how *The Oxford Companion to the Bible* presents "The Formation of the Bible:"

> The Bible is the final product of a series of stages, including orally transmitted traditions, shorter and longer written units, collections edited and in some cases translated in ancient times, and final selection by various religious communities as canonical scriptures.

Since economic trade between the West and the East of Asia was in place at that time, ideological exchange was also facilitated. The Roman Empire itself mediated a wide cultural mix through its vast occupation. Therefore, we can see how the "orally transmitted traditions," "written units," and "collections edited and translated in ancient times," which eventually gave birth to the Bible, might have been containing teachings of a much deeper meaning than the current Christian doctrine consists of.

Jesus and Buddha

The gospels of Matthew, Mark, Luke, and John of the New Testament, which present Jesus' view on life, definitely expose some clear Eastern philosophical concepts. First of all, Jesus uses the words "heaven" and "God" interchangeably,[9] which offers the same meaning for God as the Eastern traditions do: God is that Universal Force (Intelligence) that holds the universe together. Heaven being all that is, the *omnipresent* God, there is no room for another place called Hell. This is another parallel to the Eastern view that suggests that Heaven and Hell are in fact implicit components of human life on Earth, in accordance with personal deeds. Furthermore, although the Christian Church likes to present Jesus as the only son of God, Luke 3:38 and John 20:17 are two clear statements that contradict this traditional Christian claim.[10] Moreover, Jesus' teachings continue to be out of line with the later imposed Christian doctrine by not condemning the theory of reincarnation:[11]

> And it came to pass, as he was alone praying, his disciples were with him: and he asked them, saying, Whom say the people that I am? They answering said, John the Baptist; but some say Elias; and others *say*, that one of the old prophets is risen again.
>
> **(Luke 9:18,19)**

Along with reincarnation Jesus also includes karma[12] (the Eastern law of cause and effect) in his teachings:

> Afterward Jesus findeth him in the temple, and said unto him, Behold, thou art made whole: sin no more, lest a worse thing come unto thee.
>
> **(John 5:14)**

Here we should underline that Jesus did not say that "God will punish you," but instead he said "a worse thing come unto thee," which can mean that the "worse thing" will come automatically. This makes sense only if we understand it in the context of a perfectly balanced universe where all its components work in concert in union and interconnection.

To top it all off, Jesus affirms that God is in all humans:

I and *my* Father are one.

(John 10:30)

Is it not written in your law, I said, Ye are gods?

(John 10:34)

If I do not the works of my Father, believe me not.

But if I do, though you believe not me, believe the works: that ye may know, and believe, that the Father *is* in me, and I in him.

(John 10:37,38)

Yet a little while, and the world seeth me no more; but you see me: because I live, ye shall live also.

At that day ye shall know that I *am* in my Father, and ye in me, and I in you.

(John 14:19,20)

What clearer statement do we need to describe the universal union paradigm than this from one of the most revered personalities of the known human history? Jesus the Christ made it clear: we are all one, we are all gods, and he did underline other existential precepts pertaining to this theme.

As we examine the famous Sermon on the Mount (Luke 6:20–49) more of Jesus' teachings remind us clearly of karma and, implicitly of reincarnation. Conversely, ignoring karma and reincarnation, these statements make no logical sense. Instead, they appeal only to a dogmatic interpretation: the consequences for the deeds from this material life will be made manifest in the eternal, nonmaterial hereafter. The argument that supports the Eastern philosophy in the teachings of Jesus is the very nature of the union of all that is: the omnipresent God and heaven (which includes the Earth) mean the same thing as in the teachings of Jesus. Here are a few statements from The Sermon on the Mount:

> Blessed *be ye* poor: for yours is the kingdom of God.
>
> Blessed *are ye* that hunger now: for ye shall be filled. Blessed *are ye* that weep now: for ye shall laugh.
>
> **(Luke 6:20, 21)**

> But love ye your enemies, and do good, and lend, hoping for nothing again: and your reward should be great, and ye shall be children of the Highest: for he is kind unto the unthankful and *to* the evil.
>
> **(Luke 6:35)**

> Be ye therefore merciful, as your Father also is merciful. Judge not, and ye shall not be judged: condemn not, and ye shall not be condemned: forgive, and ye shall be forgiven:Give, and it shall be given unto you: good measure, pressed down, and shaken together, and running over, shall men give into your bosom. For with the same measure that ye mete withal it shall be measured to you again.
>
> **(Luke 6:36–38)**

Here Jesus departs from the Old Testament teachings about a God of vengeance and cruel retribution, in favor of a tolerant, understanding, patient, and merciful God. The latter view is similar to that presented in the Eastern philosophy where God is the omnipresent observer who honors the human free will unconditionally. So God is implicitly kind to "the unthankful and *to* the evil," their rewards for their deeds being automatically distributed to them as fair consequences. Therefore, a tough challenge for a

Christian is to decide which God is the "true" God: the one presented in the Old Testament or the one Jesus describes in the New Testament. From the previous quotes it appears that Jesus contradicts himself when he says that, on one hand God is merciful and kind, and on the other hand people should "condemn not" not to be condemned. The question is: condemned by whom? The only way to avoid this contradiction is to understand that when Jesus says "be condemned" he means an automatic, karmic balancing of one's previous deeds (a self judgment if you wish), but not as a punishment from a cruel external God.

It is, therefore, evident that Jesus teaches a much broader philosophy than the Church would like to admit. The New Testament contains clear statements to support an image of inclusion and union instead of separation and punishment. The very unworthiness of humans, which is promoted by the fundamentalist Christian doctrine in order to minimize self realization, is not part of Jesus' teachings when he encourages humans to take charge of their destiny and to become perfect, "even as your Father which is in heaven is perfect."[13]

This is in fact what Buddhism teaches by karma and reincarnation: the ultimate aspiration is that through multiple incarnations the spiritual human entity will eventually realize the complete union with God or the Universal Intelligence. In *Jesus and Buddha* edited by Marcus Borg, some of the clearest similarities between the two ancient personalities are made evident. Here are a few examples on a variety of existential philosophical themes:

"Do to others as you would have them do to you," said Jesus.

"Consider others as yourself," said Buddha.

"Give to anyone who requests it," said Jesus.

"Give when you are asked," said Buddha.

"If anyone strikes you on the cheek, offer the other also," said Jesus.

"If anyone should give you a blow with his hand, with a stick, or with a knife, you should abandon any desires and utter no evil words," said Buddha.

Grace and truth came through Jesus Christ.

John 1:17.

The body of the Buddha is born of love, patience, gentleness, and truth.

Vimalakirtinirdesha Sutra 2.

"Do not let your hearts be troubled, and do not let them be afraid," said Jesus.

"May fear and dread not conquer me," said Buddha.

Many of his disciples turned back and no longer went about with him.

John 6.66.

Sixty more gave up the training and returned to the lower life, saying: "Hard is the task of the Exalted One!"

Anguttara Nikaya 7.68.

Then Jesus cried again with a loud voice and breathed his last. At that moment the curtain of the temple was torn in two, from top to bottom. The earth shook, and the rocks were split.

Matthew 27.50–51.

At the Blessed Lord's final passing there was a great earthquake, terrible and hair-raising, accompanied by thunder.

Digha Nikaya 16.6.10.

The Son of Man came eating and drinking, and they said, "Look, a glutton and a drunkard, a friend of the tax collectors and sinners!"

Matthew 11.19.

They agreed among themselves: "Friends, here comes the recluse Gautama who lives luxuriously, who gave up his striving and reverted to luxury."

Majjhima Nikaya 26.26.

He said to them, "When I sent you out without a purse, bag, or sandals, did you lack anything?" They said, "No, not a thing."

Luke 22.35.

Then the Lord addressed the monks, saying: "I am freed from all snares. And you, monks, are freed from all snares."

Vinaya, Mahavagga 1.11.1.

If you wish to be perfect, go, sell your possessions, and give the money to the poor, and you will have treasure in heaven.

Matthew 19.21.

The avaricious do not go to heaven, the foolish do not extol charity. The wise one, however, rejoicing in charity, becomes thereby happy in the beyond.

Dhammapada 13.11.

Blessed are you who are poor, for yours is the kingdom of God.

Luke 6.20.

Let us live most happily, possessing nothing; let us feed on joy, like the radiant gods.

Dhammapada 15.4.

Jesus knew all people and needed no one to testify about anyone; for he himself knew what was in everyone.

John 2.24–25.

He was expert in knowing the thoughts and actions of living beings.

Vimalakirtinirdesha Sutra 2.

There is nothing outside a person that by going in can defile, but the things that come out are what defile.

Mark 7.15.

Stealing, deceiving, adultery; this is defilement. Not the eating of meat.

Sutta Nipata 242.

Truly I tell you, just as you did not do it to one of the least of these, you did not do it to me.

Matthew 25.45.

If you do not tend one another, then who is there to tend you? Whoever would tend me, he should tend the sick.

Vinaya, Mahavagga 8.26.3.

The evident similarity between the lives and teachings of Jesus and Buddha cannot but raise monumental questions. Since Jesus lived about 500 years after Buddha, could it be that the story of Jesus has been at least partially inspired by the older and well documented life of Buddha? Or could it be that in fact Jesus traveled to the Far East where he received his spiritual education and training? Could it be that the authors have been instructed to eliminate from the biblical scriptures anything that suggests Buddhist influences (such as the belief in karma and reincarnation) but overlooked some, like the ones I quoted? Could it also be that this intrusion is responsible for the well known discrepancies present in the four gospels of the New Testament?

Finally, since Islam, another major religion in the world, came into being about 500 years after Jesus, could it be that its creator, the ex-warrior Mohamed, had been inspired by events and teachings from the lives of Buddha and Jesus? After all, a philosophical common thread is perceivable the more we study the three major religions. However, it seems that the more centuries passed since the time of Buddha, Christianity and later Islam displayed less and less tolerance toward each other and toward the rest of the world of spiritual ideas. The modern culmination of international terrorism and war is obviously based on extremist fundamentalist religious sectarian ideology far removed from the ideas of peace, balance, and unity promulgated by Buddha. Consequently, in this book I want to provide scientific, spiritual, and religious testimonies in order to eliminate violence by abolishing the paradigm of separation that causes all these problems, in favor of a model of universal union in peace and harmony between people and between nations.

A Closer Look at the Bible

Due to many contradictory statements found within the large volume of its teachings, the Bible at large has been heavily analyzed and interpreted over the centuries, giving birth to numerous Christian sects. After the Catholic and Eastern Orthodox main branches formed themselves, Protestantism came into existence, and later many other smaller denominations separated themselves from the main stream. Regardless of its size, each one of them claims to possess the "real truth" about the word of God, about our place in the universe, and about the threefold relationship between God, humans, and nature. So from the same scriptures, different groups of people, with different views, different awareness, and different intentions, formulated different doctrines, teaching their followers different "truths." Starting by setting strict norms such as what one should or should not eat, which day should really be the day of rest (Sunday or Saturday), a wide variety of social values are the focus of each individual Christian sect.

It is interesting to see how this variety leaves room for dangerous interpretations of the biblical writings. From the time of the Inquisition to the David Koresh's sect in Waco, Texas, wars, mass suicide, accumulation of powerful weapons, and opposition to existing democratic governmental rules and regulations are extreme examples of acts committed in the name of God. The last few decades provide enough sad experiences of this kind and I would suggest that the heterogeneous nature of the biblical scriptures could justify them.

Not only does the Bible contain such a contradictory mixture of teachings, but it also omits some of the most important information pertaining to the life of Jesus. I am referring of course to the famous 18 years missing from his reported life. The Bible presents us with no reference to the life of Jesus from 12 years old to 30 years old, when he reappeared as a spiritual teacher, performing miracles, and then finally offering himself on the cross. Where was Jesus during those 18 years? What did he do? Where was he educated, trained, and initiated such that he appeared as a saint at 30 years of age? The Bible makes no effort to clarify these issues. However, many critics agree that the Second Council of Constantinople, in 533 A.D., should be held responsible for removing a number of books from the original biblical collection. Such an act can easily explain many other discrepancies found in the Bible, and it can explain the absence of the most important years from the life of the main biblical personality, Jesus Christ.

The question remains: Why? Why did the people in power order this done? How was the original Bible not serving them? An answer is possible if we consider the few remnants I mentioned in previous pages, namely those verses that indicate Eastern philosophy (karma and reincarnation for example). It seems plausible that Roman emperors wanted to present Christianity as a stand-alone religion, backed by their entire support group who would not be happy with the idea of reincarnation and karma. Being aware of the pain and suffering they have caused during their rein, they wouldn't be willing to come back to Earth to future lives of suffering in order to balance their past karmic deeds. These seem to be good enough reasons to eliminate such teachings from the Bible, focusing instead on those that institutionalize fear and punishment in hell for any act of rebellion against the imposed doctrine. However well planned their intentions were, they only partially succeeded. The quotations I listed above are only a few examples of clear references to Eastern philosophy left in the Bible.

From the very beginning the East made its appearance in Christ's life through the three wise men who assumably showed up shortly after his birth. It is important to mention that they brought specific presents, and they paid this visit in spite of the unstable political situation existing at that time around Nazareth. As the child grew older, travel opportunities to the East were facilitated by the constant trade through numerous merchant caravans.

Therefore, it seems very logical that such an opportunity was offered also to a unique and promising mind as Jesus', especially considering the noted wise men's visit. Extensive research has been conducted on the possibility that Jesus actually spent the 18 years traveling to the East. Books and video programs document many impressive findings along these lines. Especially after the discovery of the well known Dead Sea Scrolls, and with detailed information about the order of the Essenes, Jesus' travel to the East appears very probable.

One of the researchers on these matters was Edmond Bordeaux Szekely.[14] In his volume *The Essene Origins of Christianity*, he provides a detailed analysis of the historical facts that surrounded the biblical events connected to the life of Jesus. Not only does he maintain that the Gospels have been changed over time, but he also shows that historical writings regarding the life of the Jews, since they were shedding light over Christ's period, have also been tempered with. One of the great historians of that time was Flavius Josephus. After describing Josephus' writing style as full of "vigor and delicacy of coloring," with "a dramatic and vivid descriptive ability," here is how Dr. Bordeaux expresses his opinion:

> His scenes live and we feel close to the events described. He is not inferior to Herodotus, Thucydides or Tacitus in his power to make things move and live.
>
> Yet as soon as this great historian touches upon the events of the time of Tiberius and Pontius Pilate, and of the few years succeeding, he suddenly becomes full of obscurities, of contradictory repetitions, of inexplicable reticences.[15]

This is only one example of his detailed effort to dig deep into the complete scheme of the Church meant to "conceal the historical truth," in Dr. Bordeaux's words. The imposture of changing original historical writings in the long-term interest of the Church culminates, according to Dr. Bordeaux, with "the lie of the resurrection—a later invention." The fourth century emperor, Julian, went out on a limb to prove "the purely human trickery" that sits at the foundation of Christianity. The suggestion is that the Church's intent was to create a god out of a man, and to make it more prominent by introducing the event of the resurrection. Surprisingly, Julian managed to discover the remains of Christ, which triggered great hatred from the Christians, finally leading to his assassination. Although Julian had believed in religious tolerance, he became "one of the first victims of Christian fanaticism and blind hatred of all those in opposition to their dogma," as Dr. Bordeaux writes.

Based on this kind of information, we can see that the Church started to build its empire with a strong effort to eliminate anything that stood in the way of a totalitarian doctrine. Altering the scriptures was not only meant to institutionalize fear of sin and obedience to higher church and state authority, but also to remove the obvious accounts of Eastern philosophy from the Christian dogma. However, its efforts have not been perfect, as I illustrated earlier, and one reason for this is humorously expressed by Dr. Bordeaux, when he says that the scribes should have known that *mendacem esse memorem oportet*—"a liar must have a good memory."

Consequently, in spite of a weak theology, Christianity, understood in its complete form, does offer an ethical system worthy to follow. Dr. Bordeaux suggests that the origins of such teachings might be based on the existence and activities of the first century Essenes, a religious group of monks who lived in a secluded area close to the Dead Sea. Other researchers have looked for possible connections between Christian doctrine and philosophies from the Far East such as Buddhism, Zen, and Hinduism. Indeed, many traces in the present biblical writings remind us of such ties, as I listed previously. Moreover, a closer parallel to the life of Buddha indicates the possibility that the biblical scribes actually used the Buddhist example to build a convincing story. Christ and Buddha had 12 apostles, Christ and Buddha have been tempted by evil forces, they both wanted to eliminate suffering by offering individual peace, and of course, some of the most basic teachings of Christ express the philosophical issues taught by Buddha as I showed earlier (the kingdom of heaven is within, the reality of karma and reincarnation, God is in all humans, people can attain perfection through individual efforts, etc.). This parallel led to the investigation of a possible trip that Christ took during the famous 18 years of absence from the Bible. Among some truly impressive findings, a legend has been discovered in the East that describes the life of a saint named Isa, who came from the West and taught and studied at many Buddhist temples of India, traveled to Tibet, only to return to the West (Greece, Egypt, and finally to Jerusalem) exactly at the time of the crucifixion and the alleged resurrection of Jesus Christ.

Since such claims are difficult to verify, the actual teachings of Jesus still present in the Bible stand as a powerful witness to the reality of a complex mixture of philosophical and existential ideas. With this in mind it is easy to understand the large variety of interpretations of the biblical writings that, over centuries, gave birth to

many different Christian "absolute truths," which in turn created so
much separation and hate in the world. Unfortunately, paired with
the Greek philosophical system of Aristotle, the triple separation
doctrine between humans, God, and nature has been the most dominant educational model in the world for almost 2000 years. The
people in power preferred it exactly for its ability to suppress and
control large populations. On one hand, the doctrine of fear and
individual human dependency on exterior forces, associated with a
claimed message of missionarism had helped build the most powerful and cruel[16] church in the world. On the other hand, the Eastern philosophical ideas of universal union, interdependence, and
real omnipresence of God (therefore, God is present in all human
beings also) have started to emerge from the heterogeneous biblical content. Over time, more and more seekers for the true message
of the scriptures turned to those chapters and paragraphs from the
Bible that teach pure love, understanding, patience, unconditional
forgiveness, compassion, universal balance, and individual peace.
Such teachings are the foundation of the new educational paradigm
of union I am proposing in this book.

Other Views on Biblical Writings

The last few decades offer examples of researchers who put great
effort into selecting the pure and positive biblical teachings that are
relevant to our daily lives. Countless books have been published
and many audio and video programs have been produced in order
to promote new, more constructive interpretations of such old writings. Of course, once we consider the super technological age we
live in, science becomes the testing rod of any new ideological system put forth. Surprisingly, in our time quantum physics plays a
major role in underlining important parallels between the ancient
Eastern philosophies and the latest scientific discoveries.

Therefore, with such a large volume of information available,
modern Western writers depict the reality of the world in new and
different colors. The old, by which I mean the existing widespread
model of separation is being replaced by the "new." The "new" is
in fact the at least 2,500 years old but not widely accepted paradigm of union. The irony is that both are largely contained in the
Bible. It all depends on the selection process of the scriptures and,

naturally, on the intent of the researcher, as recent events clearly point out. In this respect, so many small Christian religious groups secluded themselves from the world, and we all know the tragic consequences.[17] However, a more positive and promising philosophical system, which I mentioned before, may emerge as a rescue of sorts from the same biblical teachings. In her 1952 book entitled *Key to Your-Self*, Venice Bloodworth outlines in 36 small chapters values, norms, and practices meant to enhance our potential as true, loving, and capable human beings. Some of the greatest teachings of the Nazarene, as she refers to Jesus, are presented from a deep metaphysical perspective that is much more logical and, therefore, more convincing than the dogmatic fundamentalist picture. Dr. Bloodworth expresses the fact that one should not follow blindly an imposed doctrinal path if one wants to prosper in healthy thinking and positive material gains. She says:

> The greatest barrier to individual progress is a slavish devotion to precedent. We do what everybody else does; we believe with the majority, without inquiring whether a doctrine is based on a myth or is a scientific fact.[18]

> WHATEVER YOU HAVE MADE YOURSELF A MAGNET FOR, YOU WILL GET.[19]

Many other writers and researchers of spirituality, who are genuinely interested in a positive shift in human development, have come forward over the last decades. One particularly unique philosopher, writer, and presenter is Dr. Wayne W. Dyer. As a doctor in psychology, he evolved into a respected teacher of a complete and constructive practical philosophy. His many works include books such as *The Sky's the Limit*, *Transformation*, *Real Magic*, *What Do You Really Want for Your Children?*, and an impressive audio program in cooperation with Dr. Deepak Chopra, entitled *Living Beyond Miracles*. Dr. Dyer's efforts over the years in presenting his readers and audiences with practical teachings led him more and more into the spiritual realm of life. The biblical writings provide him with a wealth of meaningful material. Consequently, he very often uses quotes from the Gospels.

In *The Secrets to Manifesting Your Destiny*, among many other issues, Dr. Dyer addresses the difference between the two current models of understanding the universe. Since I contend that these different ways of viewing life are also present in the Bible, I find it proper to present Dr. Dyer's opinion on this matter, as he expressed it in a live, taped presentation.[20] He calls them the "two theories of nature." Here is the first:

Dr. Dyer says that the cosmos is viewed as a monarchy with humans as inferior subjects to the King God. This theory proclaims God as a male, generally a white male, separate from us, as a judge in control. We are presented as untrustworthy sinners looking for a divinity outside of us, namely the King God, in spite of the teachings that the kingdom of heaven is within, that we should know we are God, and that we have the same mind as Jesus who did not consider blasphemy to be equal to God. Over the centuries we have become enslaved to this theory of nature, the idea that God is outside of us. But there is a big problem with this view: if we are declared untrustworthy from the start, then we cannot even trust in the assessment of us being untrustworthy. Consequently, we are lost in our own argument about this first theory of nature.

The second theory of nature in Dr. Dyer's words affirms that:

God, or the boss, or whatever, is not outside of us, but is everywhere, and it is an energy that is love, and that this love does not judge, but is in all things and allows us to have a free will. And that this God, if you will, is everywhere at all times, and is loving, and caring....You are what God is doing....If this intelligence is everywhere, you have to trust that is in you, and that there are no mistakes here....you can see that your essence...is that divine organizing intelligence.

As we can see, both "theories of nature," both pictures of our world, are emerging clearly from the same scriptures. Those who wanted to create a "monarchy" have found the proper information in the product of the many ancient scribes who constructed what they were told at the time. Simultaneously, for those who want to create a philosophy of union, love, and compassion, the scriptures provide clear messages pertinent to such a vision of the universe. Dr. Dyer's presentation of these views contains all the main traits of two practical philosophical systems that are actually used as real guidance by many.

Unfortunately, at least at this time, the first theory appears to be the one generally accepted by the educational systems in the West, and a history of turmoil, hatred, crime, senseless competition, and domination stand as faithful witnesses to this failing existential philosophy. In spite of the fact that the second theory is being embraced by more and more people in search for solutions to major modern problems, the present Western educational paradigm follows closely the first, the theory of the triple separation between God, humans, and nature. From Aristotle to Newton, science enforced the monarchy model imposed by the powerful Church, thereby helping to create a general human mind-set of guilt and unworthiness, within an atmosphere of material survival. Life in the West displays clearly these characteristics, and recent developments in the world of politics, business, technology, and education demand with a loud voice a drastic change—hence, a new and more constructive paradigm.

Since Christianity has long been the older sister of general education in the Western Hemisphere, such a change is not an easy one. Although most of the academic educational establishments declare themselves separate from the Church, the long-term Christian influence which endorses Dr. Dyer's first theory of nature, is vividly present in teaching and learning. The very simple and apparently inoffensive issue of praying shows clearly the separation model at work, since people are asked to pray to a God who is outside of themselves, the God of the dogmatic Christian doctrine. Furthermore, all sciences taught in schools are primarily based on the Newtonian model, thereby presenting humans as separate from each other and from nature, God being totally absent from any reasonable consideration. Other religions, spiritual traditions, and mythologies are presented as primitive historical and cultural curiosities in education, as opposed to the so called "modern and real" Christian teaching. However, this should not be a big surprise,

given the circumstances in which most of the present educators
have received their own education and training. That is why a positive change must take place in all areas of education, but first of
all, the educators themselves must realize the inefficiency of the
present academic model which is based on the separation paradigm.

God Speaks

The book *Conversations with God* by Neale Donald Walsch, can be
a very effective motivator for a paradigm change in the modern
Western world. In three volumes, over several hundred pages, God,
or to me, the omnipresent universal intelligence, maintains repeatedly that humans, nature, and God are all one, interwoven in an
infinitely complex web of physical and spiritual interconnection. In
these conversations God suggests that the existing model of separation has its roots in the misunderstanding of good and evil as two
real facets of human existence. In fact, God insists, evil is an illusion created only for the purpose of evidencing the good. In other
words, in the absence of evil good cannot exist. This statement of
duality makes perfect sense and we can witness its validity all
around us: there is no light without dark, there is no inside without
outside, there is no up without down, there is no front without a
back, and the chain of dualities leads to the impossibility of experiencing love without hate, peace without war, and of course life
without death. But even death is an illusion because life, in its spiritual essence is eternal: nothing really dies, but it simply changes
form. In this context death should be actually celebrated and not
feared. In fact there are many so called primitive tribes that do
exactly that: celebrate death as we celebrate birth, and express sorrow at birth as we do at death.

    In this trilogy God affirms that it all started with God's desire
to actually feel through physical experience all that God knows
conceptually. To me, this makes logical sense. The following experience from my own life comes to mind as a parallel: for years I
have been watching tennis either on television or at the court side,
I understood the rules of the game, and I had some concept of the
difficulty and the beauty of the game mostly from watching it and

listening to commentators, trainers, and players. However, when I actually started to seriously train and play tennis myself, I gained a real feeling, satisfaction, and appreciation for all that this sport can bring to the player, not to mention the emotions of winning or loosing. That allows me to understand how God could want to actually become a "player" of all conceptual experience held in the infinite God-Head, instead of simply "watching" it in its own imagination. In fact God maintains that the moment when God's grand desire became physical reality was what modern scientists call the Big Bang,…and the rest is history.

The large volume of explanations presented in *Conversations with God* touches an impressive variety of sensitive areas such as politics, marriage, family, optimal health, economics, extraterrestrial life, death, and of course religion and spirituality. One area that is repeatedly emphasized reminds us that God is not a totalitarian dictator, but instead, since it allowed all entities to have free will, God is a simple observer of all that is going on in the cosmos. So, if we ask for directions of conduct in our lives through questions, meditation, or prayer, God answers instantaneously through our common sense and logic, but it will never interfere with our decision. God ensures us that, yes, we have free will, but we should be aware of the consequences of our decisions. This does not mean that at the end of our deciding, hence our lives, we will be judged by some external universal power that condemns us to eternal damnation or sends us to paradise. Rather, since we are all one, we, ourselves, as spiritual entities, *we* will be our most exigent judges. That becomes the exact moment when we decide whether or not to take a new incarnation in order to "fix" some of the things we are not too proud of from our previous lives. Moreover, God maintains that, no, we do not *have* to reincarnate, so it is not an automatic causation. Instead, it is a decision we, as spiritual entities will have to make. However, from a humane point of view, understanding our existence as human beings on planet Earth within our sense of intrinsic responsibility to ourselves and each other, I would like to suggest that we *will* decide to "fix" whatever negativity we caused in our past, therefore our future incarnations are almost certain.

Therefore, on the subject of religion in general and Christianity in particular, in this trilogy God encourages us to think outside the box. In other words, we should be open to more possibilities for real experience than just one, and we should be willing to evaluate and eventually accept the idea that certain classical teachings might not be as straight forward as their advocates would like us to believe. Sounds familiar? As mentioned earlier: God suggests that indeed, many scriptures (the Bible) having been originated and preserved orally at first, then through multiple translations and printing, have been altered with or without malicious intent. In this respect one should not take all scriptures at face value especially two thousands years after they have been committed to writing. Instead, people should listen to their own hearts and become receptive to the feelings they get when they are exposed to doctrinal scriptures: what makes sense, what is clear, what makes them feel good about that information?

In this respect, in *Conversations with God* God maintains that there are only two feelings humans actually experience: the feelings of love and of fear. All the other feelings and emotions are in fact derivations of these two. Moreover, the feeling of fear is an illusion made necessary in order to experience love, unconditional love being the only true conceptual emotion in the mind of God. Another way of saying this is that we are actually all love, but we invented fear to be able to play the game of life, which without a winner and a looser is not a game at all. Here is where the true unity of all that is is made visible: separation is an illusion necessary in order to make the game of life possible. In fact at birth all human souls (those individualized God particles incarnated to experience the theoretical concepts in physicality) agreed to forget where they are actually coming from and what they really are, not to spoil the party (so to speak). God suggests that human life has no particular meaning except for the one we give it. The individualized God entities incarnated strive for the remembrance of that essential truth: we are all one, and our intrinsic goal is to be eventually reunited through the realization that we have been all one all along but we decided to play the game of separation for the reasons mentioned earlier. There is no place where one soul ends and another begins, as there is no place where the air in the kitchen ends and that of the living room begins, since there is no physical separation possible in the vibrational universal soul. In fact there is only one soul that decided to individualize itself into an infinite number of components in order to experience the wide range of physical experiences.

Based on all these considerations from the *Conversations with God* trilogy, it is obvious that God suggests that all troubles of the human race spring from our misunderstanding of who we really are and what God is. This statement makes sense once again, since if we realize that in fact, at the core, we are all united, we could do absolutely no harm to each other, exactly as the right hand will not intentionally harm any other part of the body once it understands that its own existence depends completely on the well being of the entire physical entity; in other words, doing harm to others is actually harming ourselves. As body parts are to our body, as organs are to our body, as tissues are to our body, as cells and molecules are to our body, and as atoms are to our body, so are we, the human beings, to the universe, hence to God. As we will see shortly, quantum physics testify that at the subatomic level there is an indestructible connection and a constant exchange of energy between all that is. This is the understanding that needs to be made available to all of us in order to facilitate a general transition from the paradigm of separation to the one of union. This philosophical change in paradigms will make all the difference in our world, namely in the way human beings treat other human beings and nature at a global scale. Regardless of how difficult such a change might be, one thing is certain: modern science, especially the quantum physics of the 20th century, offers scientific proof for the validity of the union paradigm.

Chapter 5:

Scientists for Unity (I)

By getting to smaller and smaller units, we do not come to fundamental units, or indivisible units, but we do come to a point where division has no meaning.

Werner Heisenberg

Scientific Ideas

The evolution of science over the centuries has been marked by a variety of discoveries in new directions. Consequently, prominent scientists have expressed their professional and philosophical points of view in accordance with the science of the day. Many qualified writers have taken the responsibility of editing and publishing such expert scientific testimony, thereby presenting a wealth of information on science, mind, spirit, religion, education, and their interactions and social implications.

The 20th century witnessed some of the most crucial discoveries in physics. Theories that explain the very composition of matter, along with the nature of time and space, marked the birth of quantum mechanics. As one might expect, not all scientists agree on one particular point of view, and there are many notable controversies between respected physicists. Especially when they are asked to express their convictions regarding philosophical themes, opinions are divided.

Religion and spirituality are two areas where some scientists like to express their position, especially if they can relate these subjects to their field of expertise. Considering the latest advances in quantum physics, many 20th and 21st century physicists have offered powerful new insights into the spiritual implications of such revolutionary work. We will see here how some of these great minds explore the sensitive territory of science, mind, and spirit. We will see how the old theory of separation gives way to the unity model, which theoretically has been praised as a possibility for thousands of years.[21] Now is the time when the theory itself is supported by scientific evidence. This satisfies not only the Westerners' demand for proof, but it also offers a real future to the merging of science and spirituality. Quantum physics emerges as that branch of science meant to bridge these two apparently opposite areas of modern life. As it has been so eloquently expressed in Shirley MacLaine's book *Out on a Limb*[22], science and technology *without* an understanding of God can be destructive, while *with* an understanding of God they are constructive and unlimited. However obvious this statement is, Westerners still want to have facts and possibilities clearly presented as tangible evidence.

As it relates to the issue at hand—namely the existence or nonexistence of God (and consequent implications for modern education)—even without any extra material or logical reasoning, the theory of probability has been employed skillfully by the French scientist and noted philosopher Blaise Pascal in order to suggest that we will be far better off as believers in God, versus nonbelievers. Here is how he expresses his "rule of the wager" in Pensees (Thoughts):

> If you bet God exists and live accordingly, you will have gained much, even if God does not exist; if you bet the opposite and God does exist, you will have lost the reason for living right—hence everything.

Great Minds of the First Half of the 20th Century

Although the 20th century's greatest scientists who expressed their views in regard to science, religion, and spirituality don't simply bet on the existence of a higher order, hence God, they seem to agree on the positive outcome of Pascal's probability statement. Edited by Ken Wilber, *Quantum Questions*, which caries the meaningful subtitle: *Mystical Writings of the World's Great Physicists*, presents essays by Heisenberg, Shroedinger, De Broglie, Jeans, Plank, Pauli, Eddington, and of course, Einstein.

Not only do they address issues such as the positive and negative effects on the human race of the 20th century's great advances in science and technology, but they also speak to the spiritual implications and to the idea of a universal connection between all that is. Indeed, the most revolutionary work in the realm of quantum physics does show a universal and continuous exchange of energy at a subatomic level. This implies that every action has a reaction, a well defined impact, and that such impact is part of a perfect balance.

Therefore, we can see the universe as a super complex organism, with an infinite number of functioning organs. As the human body is composed of large, medium, and small organs, the universe functions through its multitude of parts, among which we, individual human beings, are some of the most vital ones. This new picture of the universe is quite different than the one presented by traditional Newtonian science, namely the separation model. The universe understood as one organism also comes close to the model presented by some of the oldest spiritual traditions, as I noted before. Hence, the idea of unity, although is not new by any means, finally is supported by modern science. Scientists act as the best teachers in a universal educational system that should eliminate the negative side of life in contemporary society.

In 1932, Werner Heisenberg (1901–1976) was awarded the Nobel Prize in physics for his revolutionary contribution in the area of quantum mechanics. The essays by Heisenberg included in *Quantum Questions* are taken from three of his major works: *Physics and Beyond*[23], *Across the Frontiers*[24], and *The Physicist's Conception of Nature*[25]. Heisenberg recognized the limits of science and the fact that religious traditions cover a larger area of human life than just the material one. He addresses the very need for meaning in our lives, and connects this to the modern trend of expediency in the world, when he says:

> If there is much unhappiness among today's student body, the reason is not material hardship, but the lack of trust that makes it too difficult for the individual to give life a meaning. We must try to overcome the isolation which threatens the individual in a world dominated by technical expediency.[26]

Within a discussion about scientific and religious truth, Heisenberg also underlines the need for real moral and spiritual values in modern society. He sees an urgent need for closeness between people, especially between the younger and the older generations. Here is what he has to say on these issues:

> But since ethics is the basis for the communal life of men, and ethics can only be derived from that fundamental human attitude which I have called the spiritual pattern of the community, we must bend all our efforts to reuniting ourselves, along with the younger generation, in a common human outlook.[27]

Referring to science itself, Heisenberg maintains that the scientific endeavor only addresses limited areas of nature; therefore, we must not assume that scientific truth is universal. Moreover, science is not presented by Heisenberg as a philosophy that creates a general view of nature as a whole, and he also suggests that science alone is not able to penetrate the essence of things.

Another great pioneer in quantum mechanics was Erwin Schroedinger (1887-1961). For his important work in this new area of physics, Schroedinger was awarded the Nobel Prize in 1933. The material by Schroedinger included in *Quantum Questions* has been taken from *My View of the World,*[28] *Mind and Matter,*[29] *Nature and the Greeks,*[30] *Science and Humanism,*[31] and *What Is Life?*[32] Once again, we are presented with the affirmation that science is limited, and that there are many sensitive aspects of human life that cannot be approached by science alone. Says Schroedinger:

> [Science] cannot tell us a word about red and blue, bitter and sweet, physical pain and physical delight; it knows nothing of beautiful and ugly, good and bad, God and eternity.[33]

He continues by putting our life in an even more interesting perspective by saying that, since the listed traits are so important to us, we don't really belong to the material world constructed by science. We are spectators who simply observe it from the outside. We *believe* we are in it because our bodies are in it, and the bodies of our friends, relatives, pets, etc.

Science says nothing about our music preferences, for example, and especially *why* we like certain styles and not others. Cutting our personality out of the one great unity was done for the purpose of building an external physical world:

> Science is reticent too when it is a question of the great Unity—the One of Permenides—of which we all somehow form part, to which we belong. The most popular name for it in our time is God—with a capital 'G'.[34]

Although the universe is great and beautiful, and our scientific knowledge covers millions of years, this awareness is limited to a mere lifetime, an infinitely small spot compared to the grandeur of time and space. Schroedinger asks the most important question: "Whence come I and whither go I?" and he offers a conclusion: "Science has no answer to it."

But the answer, as simple as it is, it involves some complex reasoning. By asking another question, Schroedinger attempts to explain:

> What is this self of yours? What was the necessary condition for making the thing conceived this time into you, just you, and not someone else? What clearly intelligible scientific meaning can this "someone else" really have?[35]

Furthermore, he affirms what spiritual traditions from the Far East[36] postulated a long time ago that the "unity of knowledge, feeling, and choice," which we believe is our own, could not spring from nothingness at our birth. Instead, it is numerically "*one*," and it is in all sentient beings. Here Schroedinger disagrees with Spinoza's pantheism, when he maintains:

> This life of yours which you are living is not merely a piece of the entire existence, but is, in a certain sense, the whole; only this whole is not constitute that it can be surveyed in one single glance.[37]

He continues to remind us that "this is you"—which is a simple and clear sacred formula the Brahmins used in order to express their belief.

The words of Jesus, who affirmed that he and the Father (God) were one, and that he was in all human beings, and human beings in him, echo the Vedantic union (that was taught in the East for many centuries before Christ), to which Schroedinger refers. More important for my purpose in the present context is that Schroedinger goes even further by stating that unity exists also between us and our environment, the Mother Earth. Not only does he describe this connection, but he also underlines the eternity of the present moment as the single thing worth contemplating:

> Now, today, every day she [Mother Earth] is bringing you forth, not once, but thousands upon thousands of times, just as every day she engulfs you a thousand times over. For eternally and always there is only now, one and the same now; the present is the only thing that has no end.[38]

Schroedinger is one of many eminent scientists to point out very strongly the interdependence between us and nature.

Our destiny in an era of rapid scientific progress was also of interest to Prince Louis de Broglie, who received the Nobel Prize in physics in 1929. In his work, *Physics and Microphysics*,[39] de Broglie frequently quotes Henri Bergson,[40] who affirms that true science is actually motivated by spiritual ideas, but that since science in itself cannot pronounce on such ideas, we need additional consideration of the soul. De Broglie shows how human being, through machines propelled by natural potential energies, extended their bodies, and that "awaits a supplement of the soul." Consequently, "the mechanism demands a mysticism." His reflections on these subjects culminate with a warning (also in the words of Henri Bergson):

> Humanity groans half-crushed under the weight of the advances that it has made. It does not know sufficiently that its future depends on itself. It is for it, above all, to make up its mind if it wishes to continue to live...[41]

These same ideas have been the subject of interest to one of the greatest philosophers of science: the mathematician, physicist, and astronomer, Sir James Jeans (1877–1946), knighted in 1924 for his fundamental works in physics and astronomy. The essays by Jeans included in *Quantum Questions* are taken from *The Mysterious Universe*,42 in which he suggests: "The old dualism of mind and matter, which was mainly responsible for the supposed hostility, seems likely to disappear." Jeans continues:

> Today there is a wide measure of agreement which, on the physical side of science, approaches almost to unanimity that the stream of knowledge is heading towards a nonmechanical reality; the universe begins to look more like a great thought than like a great machine. Mind no longer appears as an accidental intruder into the realm of matter; we are beginning to suspect that we ought rather to hail it as the creator and governor of the realm of matter—not, of course, our individual minds, but the mind in which the atoms out of which our individual minds have grown exist as thoughts.[43]

To further Jeans' suggestions, let us examine what another great physicist, Max Plank (1858–1947), who was awarded the Nobel Prize in physics in 1918, had to say about "The Mystery of Our Being." He suggests that within the realm of the human ego, which is both a source of suffering and of happiness, we need basic postulates in order to guide our daily lives. Such a necessity, which is more important than scientific information, springs from the fact that one single human deed is often more significant for an individual than the entire worldwide wisdom available. Regarding the use of science to explain nature, Plank also addresses the crucial fact that we are strictly dependent on nature:

> Science cannot solve the ultimate mystery of nature. And that is because, in the last analysis, we ourselves are part of nature and, therefore, part of the mystery that we are trying to solve.[44]

Although religion as we know it is not capable of satisfying the human metaphysical need, says Plank, "Science as such can never really take the place of religion."

This matter has been studied in parallel by Wolfgang Pauli (1900–1958), who received the Nobel Prize in physics in 1945. In Pauli's opinion, "In scientific thinking, which is especially characteristic of the West, the soul turns outward and asks after the why of things."[45] As noted previously, mysticism is still included in the teachings of Jesus Christ in the West, in spite of the Church's efforts not to recognize it. Pauli underlines that mysticism is at home in both East and West, within the endeavor of experiencing the unity, treating multiplicity as illusion. His philosophical thinking was always focused on the understanding of unity in the world, a unity that had to incorporate the opposites. With the quantum theory at hand, he was hoping that the mystic unity can be better explained.

Mysticism was also a subject of special interest to Sir Arthur Eddington (1882–1944), who, for his major contributions to theoretical physics, was knighted in 1930. A devoted physicist, writer, and philosopher, Eddington has been wrongly credited to have said (in his own words) that, "Sir Arthur Eddington deduces religion from the fact that atoms do not obey the laws of mathematics."[46] Instead, what he really affirmed was that some of the difficulties in reconciling physics with religion and the free will have been removed. The new physics has helped clarify such areas of theoretical dispute, and Eddington was of the opinion that, "consciousness as a whole is greater than those quasi-metrical aspects of it which are abstracted to compose the physical brain."[47] With great humor, he addresses this idea:

For if those who hold that there must be a physical basis for everything hold that these mystical views are nonsense, we may ask: What, then, is the physical basis of nonsense? The "problem of nonsense" touches the scientist more nearly than any other moral problem.[48]

From what Eddington maintains it appears that the old conflict between religion and science can be resolved only so long as each one stays within the limits of its proper domain of investigation. However, he also suggests that the background necessary for the

cyclic scheme of physics to take place includes our human personalities and maybe a greater personality:

> The idea of a universal Mind or Logos would be, I think, a
> fairly plausible inference from the present state of scien-
> tific theory: at least it is in harmony with it.[49]

But, in the world of opposites, science cannot differentiate
between a universal spirit of good or evil; therefore, Eddington
argues, science might as well turn its argument from the existence
of a Devil.

Based on such reasoning, I believe that the harmony mentioned
by Eddington is the necessary connection between two realms of
human endeavor and is worthy of further investigation. The possible
existence of universal Mind (Intelligence or Spirit) can facilitate the
understanding of the fact that we are never alone. Indeed, that we are
connected with everything else at a very high energetic level, and as
a result, we should behave as implicit parts of a perfectly balanced
organism called the universe. The energy nature of the universe is
what is evident in the new physics and is the basis upon which the
notable physicists quoted here refer to as union. This is the foundation
of the new educational paradigm I am proposing: Instead of understanding the world as a triple separation between humans, God, and
nature, we should see it all united, in the true sense of the meaning of
the word universe (uni-verse, one verse, one song).

Albert Einstein

Now, to a scientist of celebrity stature: Albert Einstein (1879–
1955), Nobel Prize laureate in 1921, who is simply regarded as the
greatest physicist ever. Two essays by Einstein, "Cosmic Religious
Feeling" and "Science and Religion," taken from *Ideas and Opinions*, are also included in Ken Wilber's *Quantum Questions*. *Ideas
and Opinions* cumulates essays by Einstein on meaningful topics
such as education, freedom, religion, friends, politics, government,
pacifism, and of course, science.

Einstein's extensive ground-breaking work in physics, from the
quantum photoelectric effect and the equation of energy, to the theory of relativity for which he is best known, made him a respected

voice on various other subjects. While he maintains that science and religion deal with two *different* issues of human interest, it is interesting to note that Einstein was of the opinion that science and religion are in fact closer to each other than many other scientists thought. Here is how he introduces the intrinsic connection between science and the religious spirit:

> One can have the clearest and most complete knowledge of what *is*, and yet not be able to deduct from that what should be the *goal* of our human aspirations. Objective knowledge provides us with powerful instruments for the achievement of certain ends, but the ultimate goal itself and the longing to reach it must come from another source.

He supports the reality of the union of everything there is by pointing out the complex causation of events within a perfect order. As an example he considers the weather, in which case precise prediction "for a few days ahead is impossible." Says Einstein:

> Occurrences in this domain are beyond the reach of exact prediction because of the variety of factors in operation, not because of any lack of order in nature.[50]

As the "conflict" between religion and science is concerned, Einstein suggests that its main cause is the fact that some religious ideas contain "dogmatically fixed statements on subjects which belong in the domain of science." One such notable dogmatic statement is the Christian doctrine of the existence of a personal God as a separate entity, outside of the human body, and outside of nature. Although he supports the union of everything there is through universal interconnection of events, Einstein is of the opinion that science cannot yet mix into this doctrine of a personal God who is interfering with natural phenomena and who rewards and punishes human behavior. But at the same time he suggests that such religious teachings, which keep the faithful in the dark, are not only "unworthy but also fatal," inflicting "incalculable harm to human progress." Here he expresses this idea in a more direct manner:

The author at the university in Berlin where Einstein taught

In their struggle for the ethical good, teachers of religion
must have the stature to give up the doctrine of a personal
God, that is, give up that source of fear and hope which in
the past placed such vast power in the hands of priests. In
their labors they have to avail themselves of those forces
which are capable of cultivating the Good, the True, and
the Beautiful in humanity itself.[51]

As soon as religious teachers accomplish this goal, they will
realize, "with joy that true religion has been ennobled and made
more profound by scientific knowledge."

Einstein was convinced that through scientific investigation
the secrets of the universe can be unlocked. That is why he spent

virtually all his adult life trying to explain physical realities that escaped Newtonian rigor. Asked to describe his theory of relativity in simple terms, he said, "Before, it was believed time and space were separate from matter. My theory says time and space are inseparable." Not only that, but he thought that out of his theory of general relativity one could derive the so called "unified field theory," or a "theory of everything." Such theory would have also solved the problem created by the fact that Einstein's general relativity could not explain the new born quantum physics which he rejected, even though his research on the nature of light led to the formulation of quantum mechanics.

Einstein spent the last two decades of his life in search for the unified field theory that in the end eluded him. However, he planted this seed and many scientists have been attempting, ever since, to come up with one theory that will describe, and consequently, unite the four major forces known to physics: gravity, electromagnetism, and the strong and weak nuclear forces (the strong force that holds nuclei together, and the weak force that pertains to radioactive decay). A simple, but very profound idea that suggests the unity of all these forces is based on the Big Bang theory: they all sprung from *the same* source. Moreover, the idea that the entire universe originated in a primordial Big Bang, intuitively justifies the very paradigm of union I describe in this book: *everything* in the universe, including human bodies, minds, and souls, came from the same source: one point of infinite density. What happened after the Big Bang have been actually innumerable consecutive transformations and reactions set in motion by that primordial energy.

Almost as the faithful pursue their religious convictions, thousands of physicists are working today on a theory of everything under the name of "string theory." At this point in time, the idea behind it is that the world is made of tiny vibrational strings that require eleven dimensions in order to create the physical reality of everything there is. In this respect, although he failed at this task, Einstein would be proud to know that so far physicists have been employing *his* mathematics in their efforts to uncover a unified field theory. With the previous considerations in mind, it is obvious that such a theory would support once more the model of union I am proposing.

Let me conclude this review of contributions to the union paradigm offered by well known scientists of the first half of the 20th century, with another quote from *Science and Religion* where Einstein says:

> While it is true that scientific results are entirely independent from religious or moral considerations, those individuals to whom we owe the great creative achievements of science were all of them imbued with the truly religious conviction that this universe of ours is something perfect and susceptible to the rational striving for knowledge.

Chapter 6:

Scientists for Unity (II)

*Anyone who is not shocked by quantum theory
has not understood it.*

Niels Bohr

Great Minds of the Second Half of the 20th Century

The scientific efforts and discoveries of the late 19th and early 20th century to better understand the workings of the universe have been revolutionary. In fact, based on such solid scientific ground, new explorers continued to ponder these ideas. The process of their realization has marked the beginning of a new era in the understanding of the universe. Although current developments are not totally different than what had been advanced in the past, they carry more weight in terms of their ability to provide more common sense understanding and acceptance of the new universal model. Of course, the implications of such crucial ideas are impressive especially in the area of academic education, which has the great potential of giving a clearer meaning to our lives, and especially to our personal growth.

One of the better known modern physicists of the second half of the 20th Century, David Bohm, was an ardent proponent of the "implicate order" in the universe—namely that everything happens as a precise effect of a cause and not at random. As we can anticipate, such a theory will combat instantaneously any possibility of the actual existence of a state of chaos since the two concepts are mutually exclusive. As a professor at the University of London, David Bohm published *Causality and Chance in Modern Physics*, which is a classic in quantum mechanics used in many universities, and *Wholeness and the Implicate Order,* which addresses some of the main points I will elaborate on further.

Bohm was interviewed by New Dimensions Radio from San Francisco, California on some of his later works. The resulting program was entitled "Creativity, Natural Philosophy and Science" and concentrated on the present educational paradigm, at least in regard to the teaching of science. David Bohm highlighted the separation model, which is directly caused by a perceptual shift that took place over the centuries in the scientific community. While in the beginning scientists were natural philosophers manifesting their interest in the wholeness of the universe by asking broad questions, more recently specialized institutions led to a fragmentation of this interest. Consequently, this fragmentation caused the loss of connection between science and philosophy, turning science against philosophy and metaphysics.

One other significant area pointed out by David Bohm is the radical difference between Neils Bohr's versus Einstein's views on the relation between observer and observed. While Einstein sees no relevant influence exercised by the observer in the process of observation, Neils Bohr is of the opinion that the observer plays an important part in this process (Bohr even suggests that Einstein himself, through his work in quantum mechanics, arrived at the same conclusion as he—Bohr—did, but later turned against his own results). Bohm's theory on the implicate order determines him to uphold Bohr's view on this matter, and such a position underlines once again the unity between the observer, the observed, and the act of observation. Bohm illustrates clearly how order is manifested in our lives, by reminding us of geometry, music, and thinking, where things that belong together are put together.

As to the opposite of order, which is usually described as chaos or randomness, David Bohm argues that chaos is still an "infinitely complex order." This point is illustrated with his example of the ocean waves on the beach: at first they appear to hit the sand or the rocks randomly, but, at a closer analysis there is a certain order, however complex it might be, and it is caused by an infinite number of preexisting local conditions (the angles formed by the rocks, their height, the wind, and so on). Conversely, it can be shown mathematically that order can be made to appear chaotic, as in the case with fractals.

I propose here another example of ordered chaos. Imagine what you could see from a helicopter above Manhattan in New

York City. From the air it all appears chaotic: thousands of people walking everywhere, coming up out of the ground (subway) or out of buildings, only to disappear again, cars, buses, taxis going in all directions, and so on. However, if you then stand on a sidewalk and asked people and drivers what their purpose was at that particular moment in time, you would find a perfect order: each person has a clear reason to be there (hence order), even if somebody is just going for a walk. This is a clear example of the kind of "infinitely complex order" mentioned by Bohm.

Another term that describes the opposite of order is, obviously, the word *disorder*. As David Bohm points out, there is order even in what we vehemently call disorder, especially as this idea relates to the field of medicine. He maintains that if there were no order in the causation and manifestation of a disease (disorder), doctors and researchers would have no hope.

As mentioned earlier, one of Bohm's greatest contributions to modern science is the theory of the "implicate order." Coupled with his affirmation of the separation of science into individual fragments that tend not to recognize the whole of the universe, this theory assists the formation of the new educational paradigm of union. The unity model that I propose is closely related to David Bohm's analogy of the mind as a stream. Just as a stream must come from a source, so does the mind necessarily have to have a source; a thought can be considered as a water wave somewhere down the stream. In this analogy intelligent creativity springs from the subtle source, and this process is possible by focussed attention and awareness, which implicitly leads to the Eastern practice of meditation. Within the realms of such practice, the unity of all things provides us with the possibility of seeing the entire stream, as Mozart was able to create whole compositions at once. Bohm offers his scientific perspective to show our role in the world, and in the same time, he suggests that in order to be more creative one needs to see the whole stream. The alternative is actually destructive because it implies a mechanical way of thinking, removed from the source by the material appearances. Bohm says that we should be interested in living more "upstream" not with an attitude of reward or punishment, but for its own sake. Slowly, we need to become aware of our limited assumptions, which keep us away from living upstream. Our attention should be focused not only on

the outside, but more on the inner pattern of thinking and our inse-
curities, which will help us move closer to the source. The rigid
customs within our society, which are mostly based on the separation paradigm, are to give way to better attitudes of inclusion and
union by a continuous dialogue. However, this dialogue, which is
meant to examine our existing assumptions, must be one of explor-
ing, and not of winning or losing. In the light of Bohm's implicate
order, it becomes obvious that the dialogue he promotes addresses
exactly the issue of a necessary communication between people,
such that a mutual understanding of the universal connection will
be made possible. Within this understanding, people can take a
more meaningful part in the complex process of general education.

Another scientist whose work is helping humanity step into the
future on a path that connects science and spirituality is Dr. Edgar
Mitchell, who was the sixth person to walk on the Moon. An
accomplished graduate of MIT, Dr. Mitchell took an active part in
the NASA program, and in the early part of the 1970s he earned the
rare privilege of setting foot on Earth's natural satellite, the Moon.
Dr. Mitchell was admiring the quiet dance of cosmic constellations
in the clear lunar sky, when all of the sudden a "blue quarter"
appeared to his right. He was amazed to realize that the "blue quarter" (as he named it later) was our planet, the Earth, which from the
Moon resembled a blue coin about the size of a quarter (please see
the book cover). At that moment Dr. Mitchell experienced a *satori*,
as it is called in the East, namely a revelation. On that little distant
"quarter" one could find the entire history of our planet, with all
the ups and downs from all times. On that "quarter" were all the
troubles and the happiness of our modern era, with the success and
the pain, with the riches and the hunger, and with the aspirations
and desolation of all human beings. With this picture in mind, Dr.
Mitchell suddenly realized that the "blue quarter" is just a small
part in the whole scheme of the universal makeup, but it exists in a
perfect cosmic order, regardless of our personal interpretation of
the circumstances in which we find ourselves. The stars and galax-
ies visible from the Moon include our little "quarter" in a perfect
harmony, held in place by a mysterious energy. That energy is
omnipresent, which implies that the entire sequence of events on

Earth is also in perfect order and in perfect harmony with the rest of the universe. This realization so moved Dr. Mitchell, that once back on Earth, he quit NASA[52] and founded the Institute of Noetic Sciences. The institute's aim is to explore the connection between science, philosophy, religion, and spirituality, and also to explain how such a relationship can help humankind build a better and safer future in this high-technology, computer age. Dr. Mitchell's writings, seminars, and live presentations attract a rapidly growing audience in search for a clearer understanding of consciousness and the purpose of life.

This thirst for a better understanding of our purpose on Earth has motivated many writers in recent years to explore various avenues that lead to a fascinating territory where modern physics seems to merge with Eastern mysticism and the spirituality of universal union. An accomplished physicist in his own right, Fritjof Capra[53] is one such author. His works include *The Turning Point* and *Uncommon Wisdom*, but he is probably best known for *The Tao of Physics*. Here is how the third edition of this book, which appeared in 1991, is presented in the New York Magazine: "A brilliant best seller....Lucidly analyzes the tenets of Hinduism, Buddhism, and Taoism to show their striking parallels with the latest discoveries in cyclotrons."

In one particular section of *The Tao of Physics*, entitled "The Unity of All Things" Capra stresses the fact that there are differences in the ways a Hindu, a Taoist, and a Buddhist interpret the experience of reality, but asserts that there is a core set of "basic elements" common to all these spiritual traditions. What is striking, however, is that (in Capra's words):

These elements also seem to be the fundamental features of the world view emerging from modern physics.[54]

The essence of the Eastern world view is the oneness of the universe through an awareness of the connection and mutual interrelation of all things and events. In our normal state of awareness we perceive the world as made up of individual objects, and we think it functions as a sequence of separate events. The Eastern mystical tradition teaches that we should quiet down the mind to a level where we can experience the world as unity. The well known method to achieve such a realization is, of course, meditation. In order to become conscious of the oneness of the universe, the mind needs to be balanced within a state of complete tranquility.

As modern physics facilitates a deeper understanding of the subatomic composition of matter, this essential oneness of the universe becomes more and more evident. Dr. Capra illustrates this very well when he says:

> The constituents of matter and the basic phenomena involving them are all interconnected, interrelated and interdependent; that they cannot be understood as isolated entities, but only as integrated parts of the whole.[55]

Scientific study of this integration necessarily involves the observation of a desired particle, but first that particle must be isolated through a preparation process. Then the measurement part of the experiment follows. Dr. Capra goes on to explain how important the two main parts of any experiment are by pointing out that the preparation and the measurement have a crucial implication in the final result: the properties of the particle "cannot be defined independently of these processes." Therefore, the object that has been observed becomes a manifestation of the inherent interrelation between "preparation" and "measurement," with actual exchange of at least one particle between the measuring devices. So long as these two parts of the experiment are not completely separated (so that they do not influence each other, their "interaction has a long range"), "short-range effects become dominant." In such a case the entire experimental system becomes a whole unit in itself. Since complete separation between preparation, measurement, and the measuring devices is virtually impossible, quantum theory shows the essential interconnection in the universe. Here Dr. Capra quotes Niels Bohr who says:

> Isolated material particles are abstractions, their properties being definable and observable only through their interaction with other systems.[56]

To make his point, Capra quotes David Bohm:

We say that inseparable quantum interconnectedness of the whole universe is the fundamental reality, and that relatively independently behaving parts are merely particular and contingent forms within this whole.[57]

Consequently, we should see the universe not as made of individually separated building blocks (the model of Democritus and Newton), but as Capra says, "a complicated web of relations between the various parts of a unified whole." It is interesting to note how similar the mystical view of the East is to that of atomic physicists in regard to this reality. Here are two quotes from *The Tao of Physics* that illustrate this similarity (the first comes from Eastern mysticism, the second comes from Western science):

The material object becomes…not a separate object on the background or in the environment of the rest of nature but an indivisible part and even in a subtle way an expression of the unity of all that we see.[58]

An elementary particle is not an independent existing unanalyzable entity. It is, in essence, a set of relationships that reach outward to other things.[59]

From a larger perspective, one of these "other things" can as well be ourselves. In the words of Heisenberg, "Natural science does not simply describe and explain nature; it is part of the interplay between nature and ourselves....What we observe is not nature itself, but nature exposed to our method of questioning."[60] This idea has been taken one step further by physicist John Wheeler of the University of Texas at Austin, who is also quoted by Dr. Capra in *Tao of Physics*. The interplay between nature and ourselves, says Wheeler, refutes clearly the idea of the human being as an objective observer, watching natural phenomena from the outside. Instead, Wheeler suggests replacing the word *observer* by the word *participator*. This way he underlines one of the most important revelations of the new physics: the direct involvement of the observer in the process of observation. Says Wheeler:

Nothing is more important about the quantum principle
than this, that it destroys the concept of the world as "sitting out there," with the observer separated from it...In
some strange sense the universe is a participatory universe.[61]

This is a very powerful statement, and it supports the essence
of the new paradigm I am proposing: the union of all that is,
instead of the triple separation between humans, God, and nature.
It shows that practically every single human act is actually an
active participation in the workings of the world, and the logical
conclusion is that each human being, by such acts, has a definite
impact in the universal balance. To say that some human deeds
have no further implication in the overall equilibrium around us
becomes pointless. Indeed, the reverse is true: one human act, *any
act*, cannot be erased from the infinite blackboard of the eternal
universe. This contradicts one of the most powerful doctrinal concepts of Christianity, namely the forgiveness of sins. Earlier I
showed how Christianity itself, in the words of Jesus, equates God
with the universe, which implicitly includes the universal balance.
I also mentioned how influential dogmatic Christianity has been in
the area of education, especially by promoting the concept of the
sinful nature of humans as a tool of domination. Wheeler's asser-
tion suggests, from the scientific realm, that forgiveness of sins is
impossible. Since every human act, regardless of its nature,
includes the voluntary or involuntary "observation" that is "participation," Wheeler says, "the universe will never afterwards be the
same." Consequently, we see how Christianity has drifted once
again from the true metaphysical teaching of Jesus; this realization
demands a revision of the old educational paradigm, which has
been based on the separation doctrine sustained vehemently by the
fundamentalist teachings of the Christian Church.

In tune with the precepts of modern physics in regard to the
"participatory universe," Dr. Capra brings in Eastern mysticism,
which has been postulating this for at least four thousand years.
This ancient wisdom takes it one step further by maintaining that
"observer and observed, subject and object, are not only inseparable but also become indistinguishable," in the words of Dr. Capra.
Deep meditation reveals to the Eastern sage a reality where the

world of opposites ceases to exist and where everything fuses into a unified whole. This view makes our participatory nature evident since it is the conscious human being who is directly involved in the process of meditation. Here is a quote from Eastern literature, which summarizes the revelation of atomic physics and describes it in perfect accord with the perception of a Buddhist in meditation:

> The external world and his inner world are for him only two sides of the same fabric, in which the threads of all forces and of all events, of all forms of consciousness and of their objects, are woven into an inseparable net of endless, mutually conditioned relations. [62]

As the new paradigm of education is concerned, the reality of our "participatory" impact revealed by both modern science and ancient spiritual traditions becomes crucial. The implicit union should awaken in all of us the personal responsibility necessary for a more efficient education, and this awakening must take place in all walks of life.

Although to many scientists and mystics alike the "new" picture of the universe now is a given, there are still some who don't agree with it. One such modern scientist is Dr. Leon Lederman. In 1988 he shared the Nobel Prize for physics, as a recognition of his notable contribution in the study of subatomic particles. In his 1993 book entitled *The God Particle*,"[63] Dr. Lederman takes us on an entertaining journey in search for the building blocks of matter. However interesting such a trip might be, one is taken by surprise on page 189, where in "Interlude B," under the title "The Dancing Moo-Shu Masters," Lederman cynically attacks all recent writings that attempt to establish parallels between science (quantum physics) and religion, spirituality, or general metaphysics. Two outstanding such targets are Gary Zukav's *The Dancing Wu Li Masters*, and the aforementioned Fritjof Capra's *The Tao of Physics*. Lederman's objections to these works is that they "attempt to explain modern physics in terms of Eastern religion and mysticism." After my own careful reading of these books I am more inclined to say that the main goal of their authors is to show actual parallels (similarities) between modern physics and ancient Eastern spirituality, which in essence means that science finally verifies, from a materialistic point of view what Eastern mysticism philosophically suggested for thousands of years. Regardless of his negativity towards *Tao* and *Wu Li*, Dr. Lederman does them a significant favor by underlining that their content is sound, at least as their physics component is concerned. He says:

> To be fair, Tao, by Fritjof Capra, who holds a Ph. D. from the University of Vienna, and Wu Li, by Gary Zukav, a writer, have introduced many people to physics, which is good. And there's certainly nothing wrong with finding parallels between the new quantum physics and Hinduism, Buddhism, Taoism, Zen, or Hunan cuisine, for that matter. Capra and Zukav have also gotten a lot of things right. There is some good physics writing in both of these books, which gives them a feeling of credibility. [64]

Dr. Lederman goes on to express his belief in a necessary "establishment" in whatever discipline we consider. He also states that in science, the young need to be rewarded by the establishment, but at the same time, "…in our discipline, even members of the establishment rail against the establishment." Such disputes are inherent with any advancement; and in support of the new paradigm, I would like to suggest that authors such as Zukav and Capra are pioneers who push the frontiers of the "establishment" to new heights. They join in the movement for social change at the right time, with the right arsenal of information, to show that we must reconsider the existing evolutionary direction.

Medical and Meditation Secrets

One other major area of human life where positive evolutionary change must take place is the field of medicine. In his "Sounds True" audio program *Science, Spirit, and Soul* Larry Dossey, M.D. maintains that there is sufficient evidence from studies and experiments that points to a much broader picture of the human essence than we are used to. In short, the new model of healing he proposes, or the "era three" in medicine, is based on the non local nature of the universe suggested by discoveries in quantum physics. The idea is that the human mind is actually not a by-product of the physical brain as many physicists sustain. Instead, the new model suggests that the mind is non local and not fixed in time, which really means that it is omnipresent and eternal. So far, this kind of a description has been associated only with what religion and spirituality define as God. The implication of such a statement is that there is a universal connection between all human beings—the mind—which is not really individual. Instead of having an individual mind for each person on Earth, there is *one* mind that incorporates all of them.

If this is true, it can explain the results of all the studies and the experiments mentioned in Dr. Dossey's program. Here are just a few of the examples he lists as possible proof for his theory.

- A woman wakes up in the morning with a powerful sensation of pain and bleeding on her face, only to realize that there is no blood. Soon her husband, after a boating accident, rushes into the house in pain and full of blood on his face: the time of the actual event coincided with the time related by his wife.
- During the second world war a mother runs to her doctor complaining of tremendous pain caused by a huge explosion she *felt* in her face. The doctor finds no signs of such a thing. The woman goes home and receives a phone call announcing that her son died in the huge explosion caused by his submarine hitting a mine. Once again the times matched perfectly.
- In a 1970s study on reducing cholesterol level on patients, one group was instructed to take two 15 minute relaxation periods a day during which the only thing they had to do was sitting up-right on chairs and, if a thought came to their mind they were supposed to simply let go of it, not hang on to it. The results were incredible: their cholesterol levels dropped by one third, more than the control group, result unheard of until that time.
- Another out of the ordinary study showed that the number of people who died of heart problems in the United States is the highest on Monday morning

between 8 and 9 o'clock. As far as we know no other
living species on Earth registers such statistics. So the
question is obvious: how can human beings master
this? The answer seems simple: the beginning of the
work-week is perceived by most people as a stressful
time. Consequently, the mind of the person with acute
heart problems takes over by imposing the psychological state of depression that often causes the collapse of
the entire system, hence death.

- Remote viewing experiments also show extraordinary
  ability of the mind. In such a case one person at
  Princeton was shown a picture selected by a computer
  out of a huge number of possibilities. The person was
  supposed to "send" this picture by visualizing it, to
  another person about 6,000 miles away. That person
  was supposed to describe the picture "received," and
  another computer would track down the similarities
  between the two pictures. The results were incredible
  not only by the close similarities between the pictures,
  but also by the fact that at times, the picture "arrived"
  three days *before* it was "sent." This successful experiment suggests that the mind is not local and is not
  restricted to time constrains.

Dr. Dossey states that the literature pertaining to the reality of
era two (mind—body, the holistic view) and era three (the non
local nature of the mind) in medicine is abundant. The problem is
that such studies are not taken seriously in consideration and they
are not yet incorporated into the preparation of medical doctors.
The obvious implication of such teaching is that one person's mind
not only is able to influence that person's body, but it is also able to
affect other people's bodies even at a distance. To illustrate this
phenomenon Dr. Dossey quotes another experiment, this time
involving 400 patients while they were receiving treatment for
heart problems. All had been given state of the art care, but in a
double-blind study (neither the patients nor the care givers knew
about it), the first names of half of them were given to different
groups to be prayed for. Amazingly, the group prayed for did considerably better than the other group (fewer complications and

deaths). Now, one can argue from the religious perspective of the separation paradigm: the personal God listened to the prayers and responded. However, in the light of mysticism and in the words of quantum physicists, understanding God as the impersonal loving universal energy that is omnipresent and omnipotent, God has no "personal" preference for one group versus another; after all, many prayers are never "heard." This leaves only one possibility to explain the results of the experiment: in the unity model of the world the praying groups of people actually helped the group prayed for through their own positive energy that was transmitted at a distance. In other words, we may say that *within* the omnipresent God (God within humans also), people helped people, or God helped people, or we can even say that God helped God itself.

Dr. Dossey concludes his program by stating that we should applaud Newtonian science and the "era one" medicine for their important accomplishments over the centuries. In the same time we should welcome the conclusions of quantum physics and the explorations of era two and era three in medicine. Such an approach, says Dossey, will ensure the progress humans aspire to in all walks of life.

Along with medicine, the world of politics is also touched by the advancements in quantum physics. Dr. John Hagelin is a well known quantum physicist who also invested his time, energy, and expertise in politics. As a United States Presidential candidate in 2000 he succeeded to have the Natural Law Party on ballots in a number of states. A Ph.D. graduate from Harvard, Hagelin went to Geneva, Switzerland to investigate on the latest advances in the unified field theory and the recent superstring hypothesis. Similar to Dr. Dossey, one of his main research themes is the power of human mind to affect the outside world. Dr. Hagelin suggests that guided group meditation can have significant implication in any area of interest, including public policy making. He describes the new political party he founded, the Natural Law Party, this way: "a party founded on the scientifically verifiable truth of the unity of existence." Within this unity "We really have the union of modern science and ancient wisdom," he says. Moreover:

We affect one another on the different levels of human existence, from gross physical contact, or spoken word or gesture at something like a traffic jam, all the way to the deepest levels of consciousness where we are most profoundly linked.

Dr. Hagelin suggests that to get to those deeper levels of awareness one needs to pass through many layers of creation: "from superficial to profound, macroscopic to microscopic, classical to quantum mechanical." As we penetrate these levels of existence deeper and deeper, we can arrive to the final super-unified field. That is when we realize how truly powerful nature is. In his own words:

> The atomic nucleus is a million times smaller and a million times more fundamental than the molecule. Therefore, atomic power is a million times more powerful than chemical power.

Similarly, the human mind is structured in layers. Thought and mental awareness can transcend all these layers, from the surface to the deepest reality of the self as living spirit. Therefore, the power of the mind of an individual is related to the level at which that person uses it. In this respect, the power of prayer, also acclaimed by Dr. Dossey, is directly dependent of the level at which the people pray and, more importantly, *how* they pray: the deeper the awareness, the relaxation, and the communion with God, the more powerful the prayer. Within this understanding, prayer, in the classical sense of the word, should really be viewed as deep meditation. After all, prayer promoted by the Church has its roots most probably in the ancient Vedic practice of transcendental meditation.

Consequently, it seems that meditation as a sufficiently large group activity can be used to improve the condition of the world but, as Dr. Hagelin suggests, "We don't have to call it 'spiritual experience.' Using modern scientific terms, we can call it the experience of the unified field." Educators around the globe can now present the reality of the world from this new perspective in order to teach the young generations deeper truths than we have been taught.

Of course, the separation paradigm in place today must change in order to follow the new unity model evidenced by quantum physics and postulated by ancient mysticism. Moreover, the fruits of education under the existing separation model are not as exquisite as we would like them to be. Crime is consistently a problem as the moral and ethical norms in modern society are not a priority. The new paradigm for the world around us, the paradigm of union of all that is, illustrates clearly how general education can benefit from adopting this model in every area of life.

Chapter 7:

My Personal Experience with Cosmic Union

A single event can awaken within us a stranger totally unknown to us.

Antoine de Saint-Exupery

Ever since I became aware of my own journey on the path of meaningful exploration of life, a number of interesting personal events came to my attention in a different light than before. By sharing these experiences I hope to add more tangible testimonies to the main theme of this book. I include them in here also for two other reasons. First, to show my understanding through personal experience of the inner and subtle ways we perceive the world around us, and second, to incite you, the reader, to search for similar events and connections in your own life. Your testimony will give even more weight to the union paradigm I am proposing.

My 1981 Defection from Communist Romania

After I graduated from the University of Cluj, Romania, from September 1979 to September 1981 I was employed at the computer center of a chemical plant in Romania. Prior to 1981 I had not taken any vacation time or left the country. When an opportunity to take a vacation occurred in January of 1981, I asked for a trip to, then, Czechoslovakia. Since I was denied a visa for that trip, I immediately applied for another available place to, then, Yugoslavia. Now, everybody around knew that this was the "hot escape route" from the Communist Bloc to the West because Yugoslavia had direct border with Italy, which at that time was the host of international political refugees camps sponsored by the United Nations. Moreover, since the government of Yugoslavia was the most tolerant in the entire Communist Bloc, it was known that, once in Yugoslavia, political refugees had a good chance to cross the border into Italy.

However, escaping from a hard Communist dictatorship such as the one in Romania was a very risky endeavor. Ever since 1945, when the Communist Party took over, thousands of people had been executed, put in prison, or severely persecuted for opposing the oppressive totalitarian regime. Regardless of one's profession the opportunities were very dim and life in Romania was basically a struggle to survive on all fronts: economical, intellectual, spiritual, and emotional. Consequently, as I was signing the application papers for the vacation trip to Yugoslavia I said to myself (and *only* to myself): "If I get the visa, I am not coming back; I will *write* back from Italy!"

The trip was scheduled for the 4th of September,1981, but from January to September I did not receive any notice from the

The author, taken by Sergio Glajar

authorities as to my visa status, until the morning of the departure day. I showed up to work at 7:00 a.m. like on any other day, thinking that I would have to spend my vacation some other way. Against all odds, I received a phone call that morning telling me that my visa had been approved. I had to be ready in just two hours to board a train in Brasov, a large city about 60 miles away, in order to catch the evening international train from the Romanian capital, Bucharest, to the Yugoslavian capital, Belgrade. During the early morning hours of September the 4th, I had to complete the entire preparation for the trip: I had to fill out all the paper work, get all the vacation approvals from my supervisors, put together the money to cover all the costs, and catch the train in Brasov.

This entire scenario had been orchestrated by the Communist authorities to prevent us from planning ahead, especially considering a trip to Yugoslavia, where the odds of defecting were pretty high. We, the vacationers, were actually a heterogeneous group of 42 people from the district of Brasov without individual passports, on a list made up by at most two persons from the same factory, and accompanied by a guide, a translator, and a member of the 'Securitate' which was the Romanian secret police, the equivalent of the USSR's KGB.

Three days later, during a free two-hour evening visit in Sarajevo, at about 6:00 p.m., I managed to find the proper but *very risky* moment to leave the group and take a taxi to the railway station. With the little money I had left, and *without a passport* I bought a train ticket to Liubliana, a large city in the northern part of Yugoslavia, which was much closer to the border with Italy. Around 8:00 p.m. I was ready to board the train. I hid in a corner waiting for the departure time and I scouted the large and very crowded railway station hall fearing that our 'Securitate' officer could be looking for me. After all, his mission was to bring all of us vacationers back to Romania. Nothing happened and I managed to get on the train. About 14 hours later the next day, in Liubliana's main railway station *I had to buy another train ticket*, to Sejana, which was a small town one or two miles from the Italian border.

That evening, after two days with virtually no sleep, I was within hours from the realization of my dream: to step on Italian soil, free from the Communist bloc dictatorship. However, I had no idea as to what the actual border between Yugoslavia and Italy looked like, so *I took another big risk* by asking a stranger for information. The person I found on the streets of Sejana gave me the proper advice. Around midnight, after a *two-three hour risky hike* in the Yugoslavian woods, I managed to run to freedom by crossing the actual border into Italy, in spite of the threat of being caught by the Yugoslavian border patrols which I could hear a few hundred yards away.

After yet another day and a half with very little sleep, I finally arrived at the United Nations refugee camp in Latina, which was about 40 miles west of the Italian capital, Rome. That morning I signed in as a candidate for political asylum, and I started the required immigration paperwork into the United States of America, where I arrived on January 25, 1982.

In retrospective, along my entire 1981 trip to freedom one can detect a number of instances when my fate was decided in favor of a successful escape from Communism. Here are some of the crucial moments that could have prevented my trip from taking place, could have put my life in danger, or could have sent me back to Romania to heavy interrogation, torture, prison and a life-long persecution.

- First, the simple fact that I received the visa to Yugoslavia was a miracle, especially since I was not a Communist Party member and my personal views and demeanor were not exactly in line with the Communist doctrine. One possible reason I received the visa was that the senior Securitate officer who was supposed to approve my application was on vacation at that time. His substitute was a fresh graduate who was actually an old high school colleague of mine, who was apparently more sympathetic to my request.
- Second, once in Yugoslavia, it was out of the ordinary to be allowed to walk around free in small groups as at the moment of my actual escape in Sarajevo.
- Third, dealing with a taxi driver, me not speaking the native language, buying a train ticket in a foreign country without a passport, all could have been opportunities to be turned in to the Yugoslavian authorities and for my entire plan to collapse.

- Fourth, the train trip from Sarajevo through Liubliana to Sejana, carried with it the possibility of my being caught without a passport, which could have caused my arrest and deportation back to Romania. Moreover, while I was waiting for departure in the crowded railway station hall, the Romanian Securitate officer, who I am sure panicked when I did not show up at the hotel, could have intuitively searched the railway station for me.
- Fifth, once close to the border between Yugoslavia and Italy, where the natives were all aware of escaping attempts from the Eastern Bloc, I could have easily be turned in to the hands of the local police.
- Sixth, if I had encountered a border patrol as I was hiking in the woods at night, my life would have been in danger since they had the order to shoot anybody who did not surrender.

But obviously non of these possibilities materialized. My trip through Yugoslavia went smoothly in spite of all the risks and lack of sleep. Indeed, strangely enough, many times along the way I had the feeling that all I had to do was to keep going and everything would be fine; it was like a silent voice in the back of my mind saying: "Just go on, you're OK." In the end I was. As soon as I crossed the border into Italy I was safe; especially once I entered the refugee camp in Latina two days later.

How does this entire experience support the validity of the new paradigm of union? I believe that the sequence of events illustrated here followed the natural law of cause and effect. In perfect accord with the aforementioned findings presented in David Bohm's *The Implicate Order*, every single event during my defection from Romania was the direct effect of a previous cause. As one follows the trail of events backwards, one can see that the final outcome became the result of a multitude of factors perfectly aligned to facilitate its realization. I really believe that such a complex conjecture cannot take place in a world of completely separated random events, instead, the opposite must be true: only in unity and interconnection a large number of experiences can join together to lead to certain outcomes, especially when the participation of the subject in the process is essential, as quantum physics maintains. Moreover, considering all the risks involved but never materialized, it seems that the defection trip was *meant* to be successful.

That is why I would like to encourage you, the reader, to examine your own life experiences that fit some sort of a pattern suggesting invisible connections between apparently separated events. Moreover, I would be very happy if you would communicate them to me as testimonies for future debate. For this purpose please find my e-mail address here: ir_gl@yahoo.com.

In Spite of Traditional Prayer

Before I list a few cases of unheard traditional Christian prayers I want to specify what I think we should understand by the term *prayer*. In this respect Dr. Larry Dossey in his *The Power of Prayer* suggests that we should extend the meaning of this concept to include all possible methods of praying, as one size does not fit all. For some people praying in a church may seem the best way to do it. Others may feel that meditation and silence is the right way to attempt a connection with the Supreme Being. Yet others might sing, dance, and express joy or anger as they try to reach what they understand God to be. In all of these approaches one thing is common: people who pray believe in the existence of something beyond the realm of the material. On several occasions in this book I touched on the most natural and common sense perspective one can have on a presumed deity. We have seen that some of the oldest spiritual traditions, together with modern science, create an image of a non personal deity that is omnipresent through its infinite levels of vibrational energy. However, within this model, the little specks of divine energy that constitute the human beings have the free-will necessary to create and experience what they choose. Therefore, believing that one can pray to a God who *needs* to hear the prayer in order to grant the respective human wish is diminishing the very nature of an all-knowing, omnipotent, and omnipresent God. In truth that will be a much smaller deity than we would like. In fact God, understood as the universal intelligent energy that holds the cosmos together, does not have any needs. Moreover, as Jesus affirms, before we ask, God answers. This very statement renders prayers of supplication unnecessary and downright pointless.

On this subject, based on many experiments, Dr. Dossey suggests that in fact those prayers that were made impersonal and more on the line of "thy will be done" were the most efficient ones. From a multicultural perspective we can say that prayers should be simple affirmations and the giving of thanks as opposed to prayers asking for gratification or special favors in an attempt to manipulate God's will. This manipulation attempt seems very similar to that of people requesting favors from their leaders, which shows once again how a personal God could have been created in the human image. The power of prayer appears to be real but not from such a unilateral point of view. The effects of prayer can be real in an interconnected universe, but not through a separated medium such as a personal God who might listen to some but not others. Instead, we might be able to explain it by the ability of one's mind to affect others at a distance as it is suggested in era three medicine. One important criteria Dr. Dossey brings up is that most successful prayer cases have been manifested within a genuine atmosphere of love, compassion, and empathy. This seems logical within the union paradigm since through these kinds of human values we stay connected with each other and we can be of real help to those in need. In the same time, connection at a distance between human beings might be dependent upon personal sensitivity of both sender and receiver. This is similar to the preprogrammed radio or television sets that receive and interpret the information sent by systems of different broadcasting ability.

Based on these considerations I will list now four cases of what I would like to call "unheard prayers." They are events from my life and they can shed some light on the true nature of the web of interconnected events that marks the human experience.

A Church Building Collapses to the Ground

I was raised in the Eastern (Greek) Orthodox Christian tradition of Communist Romania. Due to the Communist take-over after the Second World War, and his decision to oppose the new party in power, the only option to higher education still available to my father was the Christian Orthodox Priesthood. As the first irony of the whole situation, throughout elementary and high school he was fascinated by mathematics and the "precise" sciences and wanted to become an expert in that field, but the consequences of his political choices shaped his career in the other direction. After one year of prison, not accepted by any university in the science field, my father dedicated himself to the study of theology but with the inner decision that he would never actually practice it. The second irony was that, once he graduated, he was still not able to pursue his true intellectual dream or to find a suitable job. Married and with one child, he was forced to accept the only employment available to him, and he became an Orthodox priest. Finally, the third irony was that in spite of his firm decision not to ever become a priest in his home town, this exact vacancy was his only choice at that time, and he had to take it. These three ironies are in themselves an indication that, in spite of human determination, sometimes destinies are created seemingly out of thin air.

After a few years of successful practice as a Christian Orthodox priest, my father decided to complete the painting (religious decoration) of the church, which had not been done since the church was built, over 40 years earlier. In the preparation process, it was established that the church needed a new main tower. Therefore, prior to painting it, and with huge financial sacrifices, the parishioners helped rebuild the tower. Obviously, that was an incredibly complicated undertaking, in the midst of which most of the effort fell on the priest's shoulders. Architects and engineers were contracted, the reconstruction of the tower started, and with great effort completed. Obviously, the priest (my father) and the entire community did their best under the circumstances, and, with additional financial sacrifices, the painting finally began.

But everyone was in for a big surprise: cracks started to appear in the newly constructed tower, indicating a problem, or a possible catastrophe. Inspection engineers were called in on several occasions, and one last time, at about 5:00 p.m. one day, after squeezing their hands in the well pronounced cracks, such an inspection team declared that everything was okay. They explained that it was all a matter of the church building settling under the new weight added to its walls. That same evening, about two hours later, while the engineers were celebrating their conclusion with a glass of wine at my father's house, a church neighbor came running in, out of breath, with heavy tears on her face, and drowned in desperation. She announced that half the church had completely collapsed to the ground.

The rebuilt church in Ucea de Jos, Romania

Such a catastrophe is not something that happens everyday in the world, let alone a small Christian community led by its dedicated priest. Since the technical reasons for this tragic event are not relevant here (engineering miscalculations, etc.), I would like to suggest that all the religiously directed efforts for the success of the reconstruction project such as praying and dedicating the new building to God, apparently reached a deaf ear. All the sincere and, at times, drastic efforts and sacrifice needed to rebuild a church under the Romanian totalitarian Communist regime, which in other parts of the country had ordered church demolition, were not rewarded by the dogmatic personal God of the Bible. Doesn't this suggest that God is *not* a person, that God is not the old man portrayed by the Christian church as sitting on a heavenly throne rewarding and punishing powerless human beings according to their deeds? On the contrary, this is a clear example of an event which fatefully happened in our world of cause and effect where the prayers and positive intentions couldn't undo errors in mathematical calculations of resistance and weight. I postulate that exactly the universal balance reining in a perfectly united and connected cosmos made sure that such an event, regardless of its proportion and meaning to the community, took place as the logical consequence of a multitude of previous factors. In spite of its significance I believe this was not really a tragedy. Instead, it was a precise amount of karmic load distributed to everyone involved according to an infinite chain of previous personal and communal deeds. In other words, the community, led by its priest, had to experience this event as if they had all asked for it on the invisible stage of the universal balance, cause and effect, in a world of union and interconnection. After all, the reconstruction and painting project were eventually completed with yet another huge financial sacrifice on behalf of the community, and the church stands today.

Immobilized in Bed for Decades

The story of Edwarda O'Bara is relatively well known in the United States especially due to Wayne Dyer's book *A Promise Is a Promise* and a number of TV programs over the years. At her home in Florida, Edwarda is living in a diabetic coma since 1971, and is under the exemplary care of her elderly mother, Kaye, who, for all this time, virtually never knew a full night's sleep, since she needs to check Edwarda's blood sugar level and feeds her every two hours.

Within this context I would like to mention the story of a woman from Romania who suffered of advanced multiple sclerosis combined with other afflictions, immobilized to bed for more than 20 years. She was conscious and alert all this time but she could only move her head. Like Edwarda, she was also under her mother's constant care until her mother followed her father, both passing away within a few years of each other. She passed away in 2006.

Without entering into more details about these two cases, one thing is for certain: there has been a huge amount of effort and good intentions to help and pray for both Christian ladies, but to no apparent avail. They have been "condemned" to their specific situations at a young age, with no evidence of capital wrong-doing that might suggest a harsh divine punishment. Once again I would like to say that a certain level of balance and fairness, together with deeper metaphysical reasons must be at work for such extreme events to take place in our connected universe. However, this balance has nothing to do with the assumed Christian personal God, since the aforementioned situations defy religious logic as understood in the Western world. It seems much more logical that they fit yet another pattern of cause and effect dictated not by a personal insensitive God, but by a universal balance put in place by the respective spiritual entities who have decided to involve themselves in this particular web of live actions this time around with a definite plan to be followed. In this respect one could think that the concept of karma and reincarnation might be at work. Over the years many people who have spent some time around these ladies have registered positive self-growth transformations, which might suggest a deeper purpose for their situation.

Unheard Prayers of an Innocent Child

This statement conveys much to us. The question is: how many people, not only children, pray to a biblically defined personal God, without getting any response whatsoever? So much more sensitive is this issue when an innocent child follows the advise of Christian parents and prays ardently night after night in front of the family religious icons, asking from the bottom of the young soul, only to be ignored by the doctrinal God they believe in. What kind of faith should this experience build for the future adult? Isn't this a clear example of belief in the existence of a deity artificially separated from the human entity? The alternative is much more plausible: God is in fact everywhere—omnipresent—as even the Bible postulates, and this reality naturally ensures outcomes not necessarily according to the prayer of supplication, but instead, dependent on the universal balance and unity set in motion through an unimaginably complex web of subatomic interrelationships, as quantum physics suggests.

An Icon of Christ is Smashed to Pieces

The complete unity in our universe (uni-verse) is once again evident in the following account, where it is obvious that the physical cause and effect law is at work regardless of personal intentions and prayers that might attempt to override it.

The Summer of 1998 took me and my family to Romania as part of a European vacation, and of course, visiting our relatives was a major and long awaited set of events. With our departure date approaching, as we were planning our trip back to the United States, one of my nephews wanted us to accept one of his works as a meaningful souvenir from Romania. It was a religious painting on glass, an icon of Christ that he recently completed, and it was considered one of his best works to date. It was truly a great realization for a fourth grader and we accepted it joyfully.

Even though we were not able to attend, my father, who was still an active Christian Orthodox priest, performed within the family tradition a mass meant to bless and "sanctify" the painting, as to give it more religious validity. Two days before departure, we took all the necessary precautions in terms of preparing the new "treasure" for the long trip back to the United States; it was carefully packed and set in one of the safest pieces of luggage we had.

Although it was given to us with love and affection and it had been blessed in the Christian Orthodox tradition for higher religious standings, at our arrival in Austin, Texas, we found the painting smashed into many pieces. Apparently, the roughness of the trip from Romania to the United States was too much for the fragile piece of glass, regardless of our packing care, the blessings it received, and especially regardless of its meaning.

It seems that the reality of the material world, including the treatment of luggage in airports, overcame all the positive intentions placed within this sensitive project. The law of cause and effect had been stronger than the prayer itself, or as God maintains in *Conversations with God*, we should not attempt to manipulate God's will through a prayer of supplication. Instead, we should only offer prayers of gratitude for the things we already have or we accomplish. This makes logical sense when we understand God as the universal intelligent energy that is omnipresent, omnipotent, and all-knowing, since under this understanding God *already* knows what we need and especially what serves us best. Moreover, in order for us to manifest our free-will, God will not interfere in the workings of natural law and in our decision making process. This incident is just another example of pure cause and effect in a world were, as much as we might express our wish for divine intervention—in this case 'protection'—nothing of the sort actually happened. Instead, the natural prevailed: the interaction and universal interconnection of all that is permeated every aspect of the situation, and the outcome became obvious. Notable is the fact that in subsequent years we were successful in bringing such sensitive souvenirs intact over the ocean.

Homing-Pigeons and Morphic Fields

Ever since my high school years back in Romania I have been deeply interested in raising homing-pigeons (racing-pigeons), a hobby that I enjoy even today. These birds follow such strong patterns of social living that they could serve as models to some of the ideals of human beings. Their dedication to their young, their devotion to their mates, and their passion for their private space are totally remarkable. On top of this is their famous "homing instinct," in short, their drive to race home from wherever one takes them. (Most races are from 100 to 400 miles, although there are extreme cases when some birds flew from California to Texas, or from North Africa to England.) There are fascinating stories about homing-pigeons finding their way home in the oddest of circumstances, subject treated very well by Dr. Sheldrake in his *Seven Experiments that Could Change the World.*

My focus here is on another detail about homing pigeons that I call the "flight formation." When released for flight, either for training or competition, the entire flock of birds flies in very tight group formation: they all turn simultaneously left or right, up or down, depending on circumstances or who knows what else. At least as far as we can tell one cannot say that the "leader" turns to the left and then the whole flock of tens or even hundreds of birds follows—since the "leader" is replaced every few seconds. It is too much of an endeavor for a large number of birds to "notice" the turn of the leader and follow simultaneously—for that matter many birds might not even *see* the leader. This phenomenon is similar to

Taken by the author

that of huge banks of hundreds of fish in the ocean, which many of us have encountered, that swim in a perfect synchroneity, all as one, taking perfect and sudden group turns.

In order to explain this exceptional ability of perfect group flying, I postulate that in fact there *is* an invisible communication between all members of the flock as to which turn to take. Yes, it might be that the one bird in front, the leader, may make the respective decision, but *the way it is transmitted to the rest of the flock* is perplexing. Such communication is only possible between members of the same species, as it is well described by Dr. Sheldrake in his work on morphic fields. Moreover, I should mention that when young birds come out for their first few flights they cannot stay within the flock formation of the older birds. Instead, they fly individually, separated one from each other. It takes training, it appears, for the young ones to "tune" into the species' bank of information that allows the necessary flying communication to take place.

Therefore, according to the theme of the new paradigm, such a bank of information must exist in an invisible field of union, in other words, within an universal connection at the specific level of vibration of that particular species. In this respect, homing-pigeons, or fish for that matter, can constitute part of the proof for the fact that the universal union is real.

Clairvoyant Dreams

The following happened during my high school and college years in Romania. Like most of my friends, I was an avid fan of the national soccer league, which involved watching games on TV, talking (arguing) about one team or another, and trying to predict the outcomes of games. Of course, this was entertaining but two distinct instances remain in my memory as very powerful testimony to a deeper reality than we can perceive with our five senses.

It was the day before one of the most important games of the season involving my favorite team at the time, Universitatea Craiova. Talking and prognosticating about the upcoming game had probably triggered some invisible inner chord in me because the night before the game I had a very vivid dream. It was as if I was seeing significant turns in the game, in the chronological order, a half day before play-time, including the scoring and the final result. As I was watching the game the next day I had the revelation that I knew every single major event about to take place. I communicated this to my friends in amazement and we all left it to that.

Some months latter, once again my favored team had to play, but this time it was an international game within the European Cup. The opponent was a strong Italian team, Fiorentina. As it happened before, the day preceding the game had been marked by heavy discussion among our group of friends. Under those circumstances, the night before the game I had a similar clear dream about what was about to happen the next day. In the morning, on our way to school, I even encouraged one of my friends to bet on a particular score for the evening match: 1-0 for the Romanian team. That day, even more than others, we couldn't wait for the soccer game to take place. Most of the game went pretty evenly but during the last 2–3 minutes of play the Romanian team scored a dramatic goal: exactly the way I had seen it in my dream the night before.

Some years later, while walking in a crowd of people towards a soccer stadium in my college city, Cluj, Romania, one more such experience surprised me. In front of me there were two young men who obviously were very interested in the outcome of that particular soccer game, especially since the home team (usually the favorite) had to win in order to remain in the top Romanian league for the next season. One of the two men seemed totally convinced that the home team had the ability and the motivation to win that day, but his friend said: "I don't know about this. Last night I had a strange dream: I dreamt that the visitors will win with the score of 3-2."

During this incident I was on my way to an international basketball game, and I couldn't wait to learn the soccer score. However, I wasn't really shocked when I found out that, of course, the visitors had won with the score predicted in the dream: 3-2.

Here are three well documented dreams of "things to come," capable of revealing details which otherwise were completely untouchable. I believe that such unique experiences consciously noted by people are actually only the tip of the iceberg. Under the vast waters of perceptual recalling perhaps lies a huge treasure of such non refutable facts. Without any further "help" then, it can be easily shown that precognitive dreams add to the wealth of evidence pointing to a non random universe. Indeed, it is showing a cosmic interdependence that is possible only within a perfect order and union of all that is. Only through universal connection that transcends time can a mind "see" future events with such clarity.

"The Woman with the Cow"

A vacation by car took me to the numerous wonderful old Romanian monasteries of Moldova, in the North-Eastern part of Romania. Driving was a challenge on the modest two-lane paved road, but everything was going well up to a certain point. Within the beautiful scenery guarded by mountains and beautiful trees, all cars from both directions came to a sudden stop. Here is what had happened.

On the side of the road, walking on the right side of the pavement, was a woman holding her cow by a rope, as the cow walked on the grass. From behind, an eighteen-wheeler was approaching at

50—60 miles an hour; a huge truck loaded with logs from the mountains, heading in the same direction as the woman with the cow. Parallel to the road, also on the right hand side about 30—40 yards away, there was a railway track. In this scenario came a passenger train speeding on the tracks as if it was racing the eighteen-wheeler. The climax of this moving picture occurred as follows: *exactly* when the truck was overtaking the woman with the cow, the engineer on the train, which by now was perfectly lined up with the lady and the truck, blew the whistle. The cow got scared, suddenly jumped to its left, pushed the woman further onto the pavement exactly under the last set of heavy wheels of the eighteen-wheeler. One can imagine the outcome. At my arrival the pavement was red with human blood, as the woman had been totally dismembered and, of course, instantly killed. The eighteen-wheeler was parked at some distance beyond the place of the "accident," the cow was peacefully dangling its rope on the pasture as nothing had happened, and the train was out of sight.

I used quotes on the word 'accident' because this is the point of the story. I would like to suggest that in a perfectly balanced universe accidents, or random events, are not possible (much as Dr. Bohm maintains in his *The Implicate Order*). Within the cause and effect law at work throughout the material world, every event is the result of direct causation by a chain of previous connected facts. The "woman with the cow" picture I described here is a clear example of the complex nature of such events. We can identify a large number of variables that had to materialize perfectly and concurrently in order for the "accident" to take place; we can easily understand the perfect order necessary for this event to occur. In other words, also having in mind the quickness of the developing incident, the *timing* of the entire moving picture is incredible. On this line of thinking a long list of "ifs" can be considered, with the understanding that if any of them would have been realized (would have been true), the "accident" would have never taken place. For example: if the engineer on the train would have not blown the whistle, if the lady would have walked on the grass away from the road or would have been holding the cow on her left side, if the truck or the train would have traveled faster or slower, if the lady would have walked only a little bit faster or slower, nothing would have happened. Moreover, we can extend the list of "ifs" further back in time such that the previously mentioned "ifs" would be justified: if the truck driver would have left his last stop just a few seconds sooner, or later, if the train would have been held back at the last station just a few more seconds, if the lady would have finished her morning chores only a few seconds sooner, or later, and so on. As we can see, such hypothetical conditioning can be logically pushed back indefinitely, which, whether we like it or not, will allow us to contemplate the reality of a certain level of predestination of such events, which might not be a foreign idea in a completely balanced universe.

Based on all these considerations let us conclude now with some questions. How could such a perfect timing be achievable in a paradigm of separation? How can separate parts of a whole work together so perfectly at a large scale, both in time and space, in order to bring to reality "accidents" of this caliber? Is this not a perfect example of union and interconnection, even if we are not consciously aware of it? Quantum physics and Eastern Philosophy are joining hands to support the union paradigm which can, finally, explain how "The Woman With the Cow" encounter can be possible.

"The Julee Story"

One other incident, this time from my professional life, can illustrate once more the invisible union and interconnection of all that is.

It all started during a fall semester some years ago, while I was teaching a night College Algebra class at a small satellite campus of Austin Community College, in Austin, Texas. It happened that there were two young ladies in that class who were actually high school seniors taking a night college course. Probably escaping the high school rigidity of dress codes and other requirements, they were coming to class in light attire and were sitting next to each other, which was all of no real concern at the college level, except that they were not fully participating in the class activities. A few weeks into the semester, one of the other students, a gentleman who was sitting in the front row, approached me after class with a

very inoffensive complaint. Apparently the two high school students were disturbing him at times. It is true that I had noticed that
the two young ladies were amusing themselves by writing little
notes to each other, but I didn't think it was worth addressing at
that time. However, as soon as the gentleman complained, I was
obligated to approach them. So, in relative privacy, I talked to them
in very nice and polite terms. I explained that some students in that
class were coming to school after a long work day, and it was difficult for them to concentrate in a less than ideal atmosphere. Both
reacted nicely, insisting that they didn't realize they were disturbing the class, and promised to pay more attention to this matter. For
the next few weeks things went without any similar event, but soon
enough the same gentleman approached me a second time with the
same complaint. Once again, I didn't find the situation as desperate as it was described, but I promised to talk to the two young
ladies anew. I did, and I used the same nice and polite approach,
this time even suggesting that they could sit at some distance of
each other if that helped. I received the same kind of response, with
the promise that it would not happen again. For the rest of the
semester there were no other events. One of the two young ladies
made a "C" and the other (let us call her Julee) made a D, which
was not good enough to move up to the next course, nor was it
transferable.

This was also a semester when instructors were evaluated by
students—every instructor was evaluated once per academic year.
Not even thinking about this incident anymore, here I was, at the
end of the semester, reading the students' evaluations. Out of the
entire set and for the first time in many years of teaching, I had the
chance to read very negative comments from *two* students: "This
instructor doesn't know how to teach, he should look for another
kind of job, he is treating us as high school students," and so on. Of
course, the evaluation set had been previously examined by my
department head and division chair, and I never heard a word from
either of them; probably because the two negative comments were
such an exception to the run of good evaluations I received over the
years.

A few days before the starting of the following semester I
received a phone call from my supervisor who offered me the

opportunity to teach an extra College Algebra night course at a main campus; the original instructor whose name appeared in the course schedule had to turn it down for some reason. Of course I always welcomed such opportunities and I said yes. Here I was, stepping in the classroom the first day of school, when suddenly I saw Julee sitting in the front row, right in front of my desk. This time she was impeccably dressed, very presentable under any business standards, and when she saw me entering the classroom her head fell on her arms across her desk. I didn't react in any particular way, I held my first meeting as I usually do, and at the end of class she came to me and said: "You were not supposed to teach this class." I agreed and I described briefly what had happened. She said that she was trying to take that class from somebody else, stating that she couldn't learn from me. However, since she wasn't able to switch to a different section and she couldn't drop it, I vowed to do anything I could to help her succeed. She promised to work as hard as possible, and we both did. For the entire semester she was very dedicated, and our teacher-student relationship was one of the best. But, when all was said and done, she was only able to make another D. We shook hands, I wished her better success next time with College Algebra, and, without an offending intent, she promised to try it again with somebody else.

As I was getting ready for the start of the *following* semester, at the end of the break, once again I received a phone call from my supervisor offering me, surprisingly enough, an extra night section of College Algebra at the same campus—the instructor of that course had just passed away! Of course, I said yes, and I prepared myself to teach the new section. With only a few minutes before class time, the first day of classes, I was walking towards the respective building with my briefcase in my right hand, when I noticed a silhouette walking on the sidewalk in front of me in the same direction. It reminded me of Julee. As I caught up with her my expectation was confirmed. I turned my head and I said: "Hi Julee, how are you?" She looked at me and responded to my greetings: "Where are you going?" I told her that I was supposed to teach a class in the next building, she asked me what course it was, and I told her it was a College Algebra. The intensity of the conversation was rising and when I mentioned the room number she exploded in tears, hitting the nearby wall: "Oh my God! Why is this happening to me? This is not true! I was trying to run away from you and here we are again!" At that moment I dropped my briefcase asking her if she was OK, and I answered her question: "I don't know, but this looks like karma, Julee. You know, what goes around comes around!" (I must say that during all these events I had never mentioned to her her negative evaluation of me from two semesters earlier, neither did I treat her differently than the other students.) After that, we went to our classroom, we tried to find alternatives for her to take that course with somebody else, but since *there were none*, we vowed once again to do all we could to make it work. The semester went very well from this point of view, the teacher-student relationship improved, but all she had earned at the end of the semester was yet another D. We shook hands once again in a friendly atmosphere, and wished each other the best.

A few semesters later, I happened to meet Julee in the tutoring center at a different campus. I asked her if she remembered me, and of course she did. She was now in Calculus doing very well.

I believe this is a clear example of the perfect orchestration of events in our balanced universe, where every act will be followed sooner or later by its effects. The personal karmic pattern will implicitly direct such effects towards the right person. Julee's uncalled for negative evaluation of me as her math instructor instinctively sent her right back to me however hard she was trying to avoid it. And this happened twice, in two consecutive semesters. What is even more interesting is the fact that the course sections she had chosen to take second and third time, were exactly the ones I was assigned to teach at the last minute. And these were the only ones she could take due to her working hours and other class schedule. This is a perfect synchroneity of events that left Julee with no other exit except for withdrawal from college, which was not ideal since her employer required her to be in college. Simultaneously, in spite of the fact that Julee and I had decided to do whatever needed in order to ensure her success, an invisible mental block had been put in place so that she could not earn a passing grade during either of the semesters.

Still, as difficult as it was for her to pass that course at that time, later on she was able to do it, and even better, she was able to complete whatever other math requirements her degree plan required. This shows that the College Algebra difficulty was just an artifact, an effect of her previous personal behavior, and not a permanent condition. This suggests that once we pass the effects of one of our deeds we can continue on the path previously set as long as we don't cause other negative chain reactions. The universal balance of cause and effect within the unity paradigm I am proposing is once again evident through such vivid experiences as "The Julee story."

"My Husband Died in a Car Accident"

During my 24 years of teaching mathematics I found that it helps students' concentration if several times during a lecture I diverge from the pure mathematical talk, and engage them in some other kind of verbal interaction. Of course, there are many interesting discussion areas one can plunge into, but my favored one concerns a practical personal philosophy of life, very much within the context of this book. I encourage my students to think about the nature and the origin of the events we are subjected to in life, and I ask them to think outside the box: are such events accidental or are they natural effects of previous causes?

Since I like to present arguments that support the nature of an ordered universe, I usually give some examples which, of course, include "The woman with the cow" story and sometimes even "The Julee story." It is always interesting to watch students' reaction and response, and more often than not, they will support the possibility of the new paradigm I am proposing. But one time, after I presented "The woman with the cow" story and then suggested that there are no accidents in a perfect universe, a young lady stood up in my classroom full of students and really shook up my approach, or so it seemed.

"My husband died in a car accident two months ago," she said with a smile on her face and with tears in her eyes. She went on to tell us that she was left with a one year old baby, without a job, and basically helpless. As she was speaking, I felt the ground being swept from under my feet, and I started a poor apology attempt, expressing my concern and sorrow for making her feel bad. However, in the middle of my sincere show of remorse, she interrupted me with a surprise, hence the smile on her face: she wasn't feeling bad at all, although the memory of the event touched her again. In fact she was agreeing with me. She affirmed that a short time after the "accident" certain occurrences gave her the certainty that *it had to happen*, that it was, in a way, prepared to happen. Looking back, she felt that her husband's attitude shortly before the "accident" had shown the inevitability of the excruciating event he was instinctively heading into: he was restless and totally different than his usual self up to the moment of the "accident." It was as if he new deep down inside what was about to happen but he was not able to describe it clearly, let alone avoid it. She did, finally, express her agreement regarding the ordered nature of things, and she did so based on her first-hand experience, however painful it might have been.

She left the classroom with the same sincere smile on her face, thanking me for having the opportunity to share her unique perception of her experience one more time, and to find others who felt the same way. I consider her testimony to be a great confirmation of the fact that we can and we should open the door of human perception to at least one more sense, namely our intuition, which speaks to us from the realm of the untouchable. Only through a perfect interconnection of all that is can such intrinsic knowledge become available to our conscious mind; only in unity, invisible as it may be, can we perceive realities that escape our normal five senses.

Chapter 8:

A Mathematical Model for Universal Union

*Whence arises all that order and beauty
we see in the world?*

Isaac Newton

It is well known that, in its beauty and complexity, mathematics is the discipline that connects all sciences, from physics and chemistry, to computer science and finance. It is also not an exaggeration to affirm that mathematics is an actual part of all disciplines to some extent (there are calculations performed in all human activities). Consequently, I will use one basic mathematical concept to offer a model that can shed more light on the unity paradigm.

One of the most important areas of mathematics, if not *the* most important, is algebra. Algebraic concepts, and especially algebraic manipulation techniques, are widely used in mathematical applications. The idea to employ the concept of linear equations to describe the general model of universal union came to me in an algebra class I was teaching. I was presenting to my students the three main possibilities we can encounter in the area of solving systems of two linear equations in two variables. These possibilities are: consistent (when we get one unique solution), inconsistent (when we have no solution), and dependent (when we have multiple solutions, in fact an infinite number of solutions). The three possibilities relate basically to the simple fact that two lines on a system of x- and y-axes can be in only one of three positions: they intersect (consistent, they have one point in common), they are parallel (inconsistent, no points in common), or they overlap (dependent, all points in common, hence, an infinite solution).

The third one especially caught my attention. For lines to occupy the same exact position on a system of axes, their equations have to *mean* the same thing; they have to have the *same graph*, but their equations can *look* different than each other. Such equations (the same actual line on a system of axes) can be used (can be active) in an infinite number of ways. Since equations can represent (can model) *real* life situations, there can be numerous applications in many areas all over the globe. The same line (graphically), but different coefficients (the numbers in front of the variables) can have totally different meanings, depending where, how, and when it is applied. Here is an example. The equation $y = 2x - 1$ can also be written as $y - 2x = -1$ or $2x = 1 + y$ or $2x - 1 = y$ or $y = -1 + 2x$, etc. Moreover, from an algebraic point of view we can multiply or divide the equation by *any* real number (hence, an infinite number of choices), and we can also add or subtract a real number to or from both sides of the equal sign. What we obtain is the same essential line, with the same graph (the same "physical" shape), but yet, in an infinite number of algebraic forms. Let us see some of such possibilities:

$$4x - 2y = 2 \text{ or } 6x = 3 + 3y \text{ or } -5y = 5 - 10x, \text{ etc.}$$

As we can see, the variables x and y as the main "components" of these equations stay the same, but due to the infinite variety of coefficients that we can derive from the main equation,

$$y = 2x - 1,$$

by using relatively simple algebraic techniques, we can "create" an infinite and complex world of equivalent equations, which have the same graph, at the same exact place on a system of x- and y-axes, but each having a completely different algebraic make up.

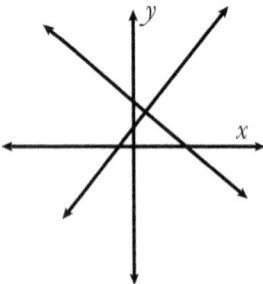

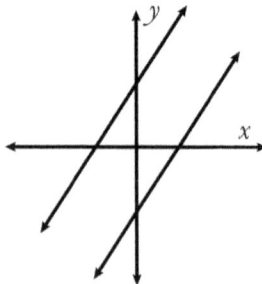

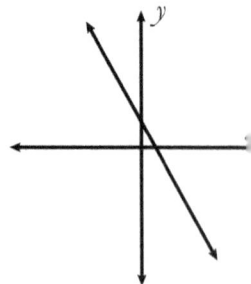

Created by David Walker

Based on this algebraic properties, the analogy between the universe of linear equations and the living species on Earth came to mind. Let me start by allowing $y = 2x - 1$ to arbitrarily represent the human species at the highest level of moral and ethical awareness. Let us consider "hs," for "human species," as an abbreviation for $y = 2x - 1$. By using this model, each individual person can be described by a unique linear equation derived from "hs" by one or more of the many algebraic procedures mentioned before. It is interesting to note that the "components," the physical elements that make up the human body, are the same for all people, just as the components x and y are the same for all such equations. The graph of this infinite number of equivalent equations is the same, it is located at the same place on the system of axes, just as the basic human appearance (general body shape, body components, etc.) of all human beings is the same. Lastly, the different sets of coefficients we can employ in order to "create" a multitude of apparently "different" equations reflect the different inner shells under which human beings exist in the world—the individual DNA uniqueness and the complex set of aspirations, feelings, desires, personality traits, characters, and talents. Consequently, we can say that each person describes physically the human species, since each equation represents the same relationship between x and y, "hs," on a system of axes. Moreover, as some people seem to live at a higher level of moral and ethical standards, the parallel is evident with respect to the lines we considered. Complex forms of this equation can be simplified through algebraic manipulations in order to bring the equation to the simplest and most efficient "hs." If we decide to let the algebraic manipulations represent a person's positive efforts on the moral and ethical existential path, we can associate each individual human being with a certain equation that reflects a level of difficulty conformed to the moral and ethical level of that person.

Here is how this works: while some people need a lot of personal improvement in order to function according to the highest standards, some equations require a lot of algebraic work in order to bring them to a practical level of applicability, hence "hs" (an easy form to graph in order to see their meaning). For example, the equation:

$$1 - 2x - 0.333 + 2(0.333)x = -y + (0.333)y,$$

definitely needs algebraic work in order to be simplified to an acceptable graphing form—after simplifications it will resume to "hs." Because a pedophile, for example, requires considerable moral and ethical improvement—work—this equation can be used to describe such a criminal. At the same time, the equation $4x - 2 = 2y$ can be the symbol of a highly spiritual person since it is very close to the ideal form of the main, easy to graph "hs."

I would like to take this mathematical modeling one step further. We can easily create one model of equations specific to each human race, and/or different models for all nations on Earth. All we have to do is to select the algebraic form we would like to use for each category in particular; it is essential to always start from "hs," as the basic ideal for "human species." For example, we can decide to multiply "hs" by about 300,000,000 multiples of 3 (3, 6, 9, 12,....) in order to represent each citizen of the United States, or multiply "hs" by about 75,000,000 fractions that all have the denominator 5 in order to represent each citizen of Italy, and so on. (Among such large sets of equations we will find some that belong to both of them in the same time—that can represent those Italians who live in the United States, or Americans living in Italy.)

And of course, the modeling can be extended even further. We can create *different* basic equations to represent other existing species on our planet. For example, we can decide that $x + y = 2$ stands for the dog species (abbreviated "ds"). Once we established that, we can create one apparently different equation (different than "ds" only by the coefficients, but not in its meaning, its graph) for each dog on our planet. Similarly, we can use $x + 2y = 3$ for the cat species, and so on. It is obvious that this analogy can be taken as far as we want, since the set of equations is limitless, as the number of live species in the universe might be unlimited as well. In the meantime, we should realize that, as I presented earlier, straight lines on a system of axes can intersect, they can be parallel (never cross each other), or they can overlap (having different coefficients, but the same meaning, the same graph). Therefore, the fact that some lines can intersect ("hs" intersects "ds" at one point) represents, in my proposed modeling, the interaction between two different species (human species and the dog species). Similarly, the fact that some lines don't intersect (are parallel) can symbolize that those respective species never interact with each other (a large number of live organisms never come in contact with humans—deep ocean organisms for example).

Let us examine now how this idea can add to the foundation of the unity paradigm. It is important to realize that this algebraic model suggests that although human beings are definitely different from each other, as their inner individual form is concerned, they are connected at a deeper level through their *final* existential meaning. As all individual lines in the "hs" set are different through their coefficients (the numbers involved in the respective equations), they are united in meaning through their unique graph. One can also say that for human beings the universal connection is firmly established by the deep meaning of human life as a "graph" in the general scheme of things.

However, we should investigate further: is there something of substance that actually connects everything? As I presented earlier, great scientists and researchers point towards the most subtle level of energy, while the spiritual masters remind us of the omnipresent God, the Universal Intelligence, or the Universal Mind. Considering different linear forms for other live species, as we saw earlier, the unity model is evident algebraically once again by the balance, the "intelligence" behind the concept of equation. In every equation, the left hand side must always be equal to the right hand side. In the meantime we can switch terms from one side to the other and apply other algebraic manipulations but only in such a way that the eternal balance is preserved. Therefore, *through the meaning of the equation itself, we* give it power or a certain kind of invisible energy, which will always keep it in balance. Consequently, equations act as intelligent entities in their own universe, just as human beings do. I underlined the word *we* because *we* are the ones who give equations that energy by investing some of our own energy in their existence, therefore, in their function and in their meaning. We can see that *we are in them*; equations would not exist outside and independent of us, human beings.

Now let us go back to the original analogy. Who sees through our eyes? Who feels pain or joy? The same circumstance can produce different results in different human beings. Why? The answer comes from the understanding that, alone, the physical components of our bodies are not capable of interpreting the surrounding reality, just as the variables x and y, associated with any combination of real numbers, cannot produce the graph of any equation without the sensitive meaning that comes from the algebraic intelligent arrangement *we* conceive. Moreover, *we decide* to bring the equation of the line from the conceptual realm to the physical universe by drawing a system of axes and graphing the line on it. This can be similar to the incarnation each human being *decides* to take in order to experience a certain physical life.

From a physical perspective real numbers, systems of axes, the variables x and y, and all the rest of the mathematical apparatus are, after all, an illusion, an abstraction. Every single mathematical concept is an invention of the human mind in the pursuit of order and relationships in the world around us. We can see them at work although they don't exist physically independent of our perception; they function through their properties and qualities which we give them. The same seems to hold true so far as the material world of forms is concerned, ourselves included. Some religious and spiritual traditions have postulated the illusory nature of our world throughout the ages. Now, in recent time, science, through quantum physics, proves this to be actually true, and does so by showing that the atom, as an indivisible material entity, does not exist. Instead, science points toward the fact that even the smallest particle is a conglomerate of other elements that can assume either a wave or a particle manifestation, depending on the method of observation. This simple fact underlines the actual nature of the universe as being pure energy, whose implicit intelligence structures and organizes it in apparent forms, similarly to what we do by graphing lines on a system of axes. That intelligence is universal, therefore, it is also within ourselves, for only this way can *we* create equations of lines, or—why not—can we create our own physical bodies.

I would like to point out one last parallel between linear equations and human life in regards to this mathematical model of unity. We use a large variety of lines (linear equations) in our day-by-day applications but only one mathematical concept—that of the "Equation." This concept "materializes" through human awareness and infinitely divides itself into all possible individual equations. The same can hold true regarding our own existence, together with the existence of all other living species in the universe. The universal mind, in the pursuit of understanding itself, creates the material world, implicitly building an infinite number of levels of awareness, and looks for familiar patterns through numerous eyes. United at the source, physically *we* are the eyes, and metaphysically *we* are the awareness of the universe that interprets the experiences we go through.

Chapter 9:

Needed Shift—Secular to Sacred Education

*We must therefore take account of this changeable nature
of things and of human institutions, and prepare for them
with enlightened foresight.*

Pope Pius XI

Previously we saw how religious belief, scientific precepts, and a variety of philosophical ideas contribute to the formation of any system of thought. In the beginning Christianity was pushed by the separation doctrine towards the Greek natural philosophy which searched for solid building blocks as the core components of matter. During the 20th century, due to developments in quantum physics, scientific researchers began to see a new light even in the dogmatic Christian tradition. Moreover, Eastern philosophy and spirituality, although ancient, attracted more attention especially when quantum theory seemed to finally verify Hindu, Buddhist, or Taoist postulates. Consequently, many writers, scientists, clergy, and modern philosophers have started a fruitful dialogue on these important existential issues. Books, audio tapes, CDs, videotapes and DVDs together with live presentations at different conferences have been produced, all in the noble effort to propose new and more constructive solutions to existing problems in our modern world.

Such is the live dialogue between Matthew Fox, a Dominican priest, and Rupert Sheldrake, a professor of biology at Cambridge.[65] On one hand we have Matthew Fox, who has been known for his opposition to rigid Catholic doctrine for which he was silenced by the Vatican for one year, 1989–1990, and on the other hand we have Dr. Rupert Sheldrake, well known for his important contribution to science, proposing the morphogenetic fields as the form generators in the plant and animal kingdoms. The discussion goes back and forth between the two respected thinkers on issues ranging from the theme of a resacralization of nature, to images of God and morphic resonance.

In search for a meaningful mysticism as a better interpretation of the universe, Matthew Fox arrived at the writings of the 13th century Saint Thomas Aquinas who was first condemned three times before later being canonized by the Catholic Church. Fox underlines that not many Church authorities are willing to admit the mystical tradition evident in the teachings of Jesus, who in his opinion, was a mystic. He presents his own work as being an effort in search of a relationship between politics and mysticism. He concludes that what brings them together is the concept of compassion. In terms of science and spirituality he quotes Aquinas, who said, "Science without love is puffed up," and in regard to art, he quotes Picasso, who said, "I am seeking a new language for art."

In this book, I am seeking a new paradigm for understanding the world around us—as Matthew Fox expresses when he says that he is seeking a new language for theology, spirituality, and education. We should amend our existing educational model in the light of all the great evidence of the order and interconnectedness of the universe. To make such an amendment real, we need to rediscover the sense of sacredness in nature. Therefore, one major step forward will be a much needed show of respect for all living forms whom we share this planet with, and an appreciation for any open dialogue between scientists who are interested in this kind of research.

Matthew Fox has found good company in the person of Dr. Sheldrake, who affirms that the German poet Goethe inspired him to look for a kind of science where the observer's direct experience and interaction with the observed phenomena is not in conflict, but is complementary to the research process. Consequently, he started to search for a more holistic science that would unify intuition, reason, and sensory experience. After 10 years of extensive research on the development of plants, Sheldrake arrived at the conclusion that the existing mechanistic model of nature always crashed into a brick wall. Not loosing hope, he discovered a movement in the scientific community called holistic science, which started in the 1920s. This led him to explore the reality of some organizing fields in animals and plants, fields that were responsible for shaping the forms of organisms, similar to Earth's magnetic field. Furthermore, he theorized that a kind of memory inherent in these fields is responsible for preserving the detailed characteristics of each species. After working in the agricultural fields of India, while pursuing his dreams, Sheldrake became interested in Hindu mysticism, even though he went to India as an atheist. Within such an environment he arrived at the conclusion that his native Christian tradition also included evident mystical teachings. Sounds familiar? This realization had a definite impact on his future books, such as *The Presence of the Past* and his 1993 work, *The Rebirth of Nature*. The latter deals with the nature of nature, underlining the fact that through science itself we are rediscovering the life of nature.

As opposed to the Western depressing and pessimistic view of the universe—a machine running out of steam—Sheldrake proposes a new model, namely a continuously developing organism. He connects his ideas to the quantum theory, which in the new cosmology allows nature to be creative. In this model, the building blocks of nature, the atoms, are not rigid and inert, but are active processes—matter becoming, therefore, a process not a thing. We can see, then, that through modern physics the new image of the material universe is that of energy and fields that are more fundamental than matter. This view gives a new sense of life to nature, Earth itself appearing as a living organism in the universe at large. Consequently, animals and plants (including the human race) are considered true organisms, not preprogrammed machines.

This new vision has definite implications in the understanding of nature and God. Sheldrake points out that in a mechanical world, God, made in the image of a technological man, is the machine maker, as Descartes and Newton postulated. In this model God starts the machine, keeps it going, and occasionally intervenes by suspending the natural laws in order to bring about miracles; we can see how such an interpretation becomes less and less popular in modern society. On the other hand, in a living universe where God is in everything that is, we need an image of a different God, a living and truly omnipresent God who will raise the sacredness of natural world. As Sheldrake points out, "There is no sacredness in machinery," and it is also difficult to identify a spiritual presence in a mechanistic universe.

Along these lines Matthew Fox maintains that the sense of awe in nature needs to make a comeback. The mystical aspect of the universe should remind us that every organ in our bodies is a mystery and that every being we see is a mystery. Therefore, we need to change our relationship with Earth itself by recognizing that time and space are sacred, and by showing reverence to the sustainer of life, the universal living and omnipresent energy we call God. As a parallel to Fox's suggestion, Sheldrake presents the two main relationships existing between humans on one hand, and animals and plants on the other. Considered as machines, animals and plants are treated simply as sources of food on an industrial scale. This is the traditional model in the materialistic Western world. In contrast, by recognizing the sacredness of nature, we can develop a closer relationship with animals and plants (for example, many raise animals as pets, and grow flower gardens only for the beauty they offer).

On a larger scale, over many centuries, in some cultures, not only animals and plants were treated as sacred, but also certain places in the world became centers of pilgrimage. However, the expansion of the Protestant Reformation in the West diminished considerably the number of such sacred places. A good example of this development is what has occurred in North and South Americas. Once these territories were occupied by the European Christians (Protestants and Catholics alike), the old sacred places venerated by the native civilizations were ignored and often destroyed, along with entire libraries of information on the characteristics of the respective societies. In fact, in Central and South America Catholic churches have been built over the ruins (the sturdy foundations) of previous native temples. In spite of such a treatment of sacred places, humankind still longed for something to fill its inner need for unique places in nature. That is in part how tourism was born. Sheldrake suggests that a shift back, from commercial tourism, to pilgrimage, to sacred places, is needed if we are to preserve nature and amend the quality of life on Earth.

On this issue, Matthew Fox underlines that in the United States the wilderness (the national parks) attracts people by heart. There has to be an inner connectivity and a sense of vulnerability that characterizes such pilgrimage. The sense of constant rush that describes modern tourism needs to be replaced by heart work and compassion for the places of reverence. In accordance with all major mystical traditions, Fox reminds us that spirits do dwell in spaces, animals, and plants. This should give birth to a new theology in the West, a new language for spirituality that recognizes the angelic and the spirit world. He maintains that at this point in time, the mechanistic view is taught not only in the laic academic institutions, but also in the seminaries. Consequently, theologians are not comfortable talking about angels, spirits, and "little people." This contributes to an even deeper separation between people, especially considering those who will not be able to place the meaning of their personal spiritual experiences in a proper frame of understanding.

Matthew Fox further addresses the issue of time as a sacred celebration by mentioning the ancient tradition of dedicating a 7th part of our time to rest and contemplation of nature. Not only that, but I suggest that we should also use this special time, the sabbatical, to explore the unity of the universe and to reconnect to our source of existence. Fox says that such a use of our time might help us transcend the Western "mechanistic and compulsive" lifestyle and enjoy more of a festive existence—we should take time "to be human."

Rupert Sheldrake parallels these views by saying that even the ancient seasonal festivals, where entire communities were celebrating together, have been lost. This, he explains, is a direct consequence of a shift in the perception of the heavens. In ancient cultures, the sky was understood as the abode, the heaven, where stars and planets were alive as angelic beings, which offered a much needed sacredness to nature and the heavens. Today, science sees the sky as inert matter; therefore, NASA sends its spaceships into a desacralized and totally secularized heaven. Here Sheldrake makes a very important point by reminding us that if God is omnipresent, as all major religions maintain, then 99.999...% of God is in the sky, since Earth is such a minuscule component of the cosmos. Used so strongly by the Church to remove God from humans and nature, this theological claim contributes heavily to the rigid doctrine of separation that penetrates deeply into the existing existential paradigm in the West. Regarding this statement, I would like to note that the Biblical claim that God is in heaven gives a new meaning to Dr. Sheldrake's observation: of course God is in heaven, but we should amend this statement by saying "mostly in heaven," since the Earth is part of heaven, God is also on and in the Earth, human beings included.

As a continuation of this discussion on the meaning and the reverence of heaven in our lives, Fox refers to a statement made by the 13th century theologian Aquinas, who said that the human being is not the most excellent thing in the universe; the most excellent thing in the universe is the universe. At this point Fox guides our attention to the imbalances human beings incur in nature. As an example, he reminds us of the notorious environmental damage we inflict to the ozone layer. He underscores that we generally ignore the fact that we share the Earth with innumerable other species, acting as if we were the most excellent thing in the universe. The union paradigm I propose in this book becomes once again obvious since every single life form on our planet breathes the same air. With each breath, we actually exchange countless atoms with our environment, and since the life sustaining air is recycled and is being circulated around the globe by currents and winds, we can clearly see the union from a very practical and physical perspective. The same can be said about water. In fact, Dr. Deepak Chopra M.D., a renown medical authority, maintains that there is scientific evidence to support this claim.

Within the picture of the obvious union, and in order to connect the physical part of the universe to its divine nature, Matthew Fox cites Aquinas once more. Six centuries ago Aquinas offered an impressive list of images and names of God, all present in the Christian scriptures. These images and names of God suggest that God is good, beautiful, wise, beloved, God of Gods, holy, eternal manifest, wisdom, intellect, reason, universal knowledge, king of kings, virtue, powerful, ancient of days, without age, justice, salvation, magnitude, exceeding all things, in minds, in hearts, in spirit, in bodies, in heaven and on Earth, at the same time in all places, involved in the world, above the world, above the heavens, super celestial, super substantial, the Sun, a constellation or a star, fire, water, air, the elements, clouds, rocks, and stones. Based on such a revealing list Aquinas powerfully affirms that every being is an image of God, a book about God, and a revelation of God. However, says Aquinas, the mystery remains: God is all these things, but not any of them in particular. God is above all these things. This statement does remind us of the quantum picture of the universal union unveiled by modern science.

Therefore, Sheldrake, as a biologist, continues the dialogue by addressing one of the images of God mentioned on Aquinas' list, namely the elements. He points out that modern science gives a deeper understanding of the elements, and he postulates that the third component of the trinity, the Logos, is actually the formative principle of nature, the morphic fields. The unity of all things is also evident in Sheldrake's vision when he says that energy *is* the universal moving cause, being omnipresent, with no gender differentiation—hence it can take the name God.

Divinity as field and energy is seen by Sheldrake to be responsible for the manifestation of the physical form. He explains how morphic resonance is being built on the similarities manifested in each species. The morphic fields, where such resonance takes place, are collecting all the information pertaining to the respective species.[66] Concerning human beings, Sheldrake's view implies that what we call memory is not stored in our brains, but that our brains act more like TV receivers, tuning into the resonance of the respective fields. He points out existing evidence, as laboratory experiments show that rats, for example, that learned to perform a certain task, made it much easier and faster for other rats at remote locations to learn the same task. Another event that apparently speaks to the validity of Sheldrake's theory is the acclaimed "hundredth monkey" phenomena,[67] where when a certain number of monkeys (called the critical number) learned one trick over a period of time, other monkeys hundreds of miles away gained access to the same knowledge in a much shorter time.

Of course, one cannot but think of the possible implications of Sheldrake's theory in human teaching and learning; children learning language and sociopolitical behaviors, for example. According to his hypothesis, we all "tune in" the same resonance. This means that we all contribute to the content of the field and we all can use it according to our individual receptivity. As past contributions to a field, rituals can easily be seen in all religious traditions. People follow a ritual as close as possible to the way it was performed the first time: actions, words, songs are kept as similar as possible to the originals. This way, not only are we united with the present people who practice those rituals, but we also attempt to unite ourselves with those who practiced it in the past, preferably with the originators of the respective ritual.

Matthew Fox suggests that, besides religious rituals, social rituals can be viewed as habits that belong to positive or negative morphic fields. The heavy Western habit of consumerism has contributed to a depreciation of goods and commodities. Consequently, people take for granted many aspects of life, and often make the error of promoting negative rituals instead of positive ones. Fox encourages us to become aware of our daily habits (rituals), especially because if we are not engaged in positive rituals, most likely we are engaged in negative ones. He adds that healthy rituals are usually much cheaper and safer than unhealthy ones.

Dr. Sheldrake expands on this issue by warning us that morphic resonance has no moral filter. Therefore, if enough people (the critical number) practice one unhealthy habit, it is very likely that in a short time many more people will adopt it. This also holds true for the practice of a healthy ritual. He maintains that, since morphic resonance is not material as we presently understand the material world to be, our thoughts have the same impact on the morphic fields as any words or actions will have. More than that, our attitudes can definitely affect other people through morphic resonance. Consequently, we should exercise more self-control, with a greater sense of responsibility over everything we think, say, and do, in order to minimize the creation of negative habits for present and future generations. Sheldrake reminds us that although it was meant as a creative process, it was through such habitual thinking that the mechanistic view of the universe was itself established. Today, with the help of all the advances in science there is hope for the creation of a more realistic model for the understanding of the cosmos. He hopes that new and more creative ideas, repeated often enough, will become habits, rituals for a better and more constructive life on Earth.

On the issue of creativity both Fox and Sheldrake are of the opinion that the process responsible for the "creation" of the universe was not a limited six-day event in time. They suggest that creation is an ongoing reality, and we are engaged in this process most of the time unconsciously. Therefore, we are actually co-creating, participating continuously in the renewing of the universe. However, in order to make this process "healthy and safe," we also need to remember that we are "the compassion of God," as Matthew Fox quotes Jesus Christ.

As the "new language" for science, spirituality, and education both Fox and Sheldrake are seeking a language of inclusion, of union between people, of love and respect for nature and the divine, all in an effort to make life on Earth more humane, in contrast to the outcomes promoted by the mechanistic model. The subtle combination of the spiritual and scientific views advanced by these two great thinkers comes as a substantial contribution to the new educational paradigm of union that I set forth in this book.

Chapter 10:

Wide Support for Unity

A good problem statement often includes: (a) what is known, (b) what is unknown, and (c) what is sought.

Edward Hodnett

Channels of Information

Regardless of historical conditions, there have always been those who elected to pursue with total dedication the search for the meaning of life. As a result, we are fortunate today to benefit from their philosophical contributions. Therefore, in the following I would like to examine a number of available works, some that I have already cited, that can offer further sources of information on the subject at hand, namely the union paradigm.

From the time of the Bible into the 21st century, we have inherited a tremendous volume of work that can serve those who are searching for answers to intriguing existential questions. A closer look at the existing educational paradigm in the West shows that in spite of the heterogeneous nature of the population, important philosophical ideas from other parts of the world have not yet been assimilated. Within a conservative atmosphere, ideas that otherwise might offer clues to unanswered existential questions have been kept out. The freedom and peace we presently enjoy in this part of the world makes the exploration of other educational avenues possible.

Since this book is set to construct a new existential paradigm, such alternatives become the central stage for research and investigation. I am convinced that the failure to understand who we really are and what we are doing in this world creates the opportunity and the motivation for crime and other ills in our society. Based on reason, logic, philosophical debate, and scientific research, many alternative sources offer revolutionary information that, if incorporated properly in a consistent educational system, may solve some of the major problems we face today.

Not only books and magazines are abundantly available, but also books on tape, videos and DVD programs make one's search easier, faster, and more enjoyable. Indeed, many companies flourish by offering audio and video programs in the area of self growth, self-help, and self-improvement. Pressed by time, our driving hours can now be transformed into a learning experience, and our cars can really be called "universities on wheels."

On top of all these alternative means of education we should mention the most familiar one: television programs. With the rapid technological advancement in the television industry specialized channels such as The Learning Channel (TLC), History and Discovery channels, offer a large and meaningful variety of educational opportunities. If we add the Internet, we realize that we have selective access to the crucial knowledge we need to build a better future.

Significant Publications

Since personal education is accomplished through a variety of means we can anticipate an impressive volume of work on the subject of human development. From ancient religious and spiritual writings to the most recent studies on human behavior, educational ideas are clustered around the noble ideal of building perennial values. Prestigious authors offer important insight into the understanding of human attitudes and actions. Many studies bring into the larger picture of education solid scientific research. To a Westerner this is exactly the desired path, since we prefer consistent and verifiable proof for any theory.

Unfortunately this is not always the case. For example, Christianity has such a strong hold world-wide, but it does so mostly by faith, which is the main vehicle for implementing its teachings. The Bible, therefore, with all its modern sectarian interpretations, requires that kind of unquestioning faith.

In addition to the Bible, there is other important religious and spiritual heritage from different parts of the world that is gaining

Western acceptance. India, for example, is one of the prominent sources of spiritual traditions some of which date back thousands of years before Christ. As we have seen earlier, an interesting aspect of these traditions is that their main teachings appear to be the closest to what modern quantum physics unveils. In one of his memorable interviews, the late American historian of religion, Joseph Campbell, suggests that Buddhism is the religion that incorporates those spiritual teachings that are most suitable to a world-wide religion.

An impressive study of how God is viewed around the world is the 1995 book *God In All Worlds: An Anthology of Contemporary Spiritual Writing*, edited and introduced by Lucinda Vardey. Themes such as Contemplating God, Looking for Meaning and the Way, The Spiritual Experience, The Hidden Face of God, Being for God, Doing for God, The Spiritual Age, and Emerging World from this impressive work are approached by well known personalities in disciplines ranging from religion and spirituality to science and philosophy. Mother Teresa, Matthew Fox, J. Krishnamurti, The Dalai Lama, Albert Einstein, David Bohm, Joseph Campbell, and Aldous Huxley are just a few of the influential thinkers included in Vardey's anthology.

During the last few decades more and more works have been published on the parallels between science and spirituality. Gary Zukav's book *The Dancing Wu Li Masters* is representative for the effort that puts quantum mechanics and relativity theory into common sense terms. *The New Story of Science* by Robert M. Augros and George N. Stanciu, explains "how the new cosmology is reshaping our view of mind, art, God and ourselves." It is evident that without an understanding of ourselves we cannot successfully establish an educational paradigm to peacefully carry us into the future ("Know thyself," says the Bible). In 1993 a new edition of the 1960 *Psycho-Cybernetics* by Maxwell Maltz was published, this time entitled *Psycho-Cybernetics 2000* and written by Bobbe Sommer, Ph.D. The intent is to help us take control of our lives and achieve success and happiness.

Since the children of today will be the parents of tomorrow, we need both to learn and to teach health. Within the old educational paradigm, health is generally understood to be simply the absence of illness. However, the holistic understanding of health is that of well-being—the absence of illness, designing a lifestyle meant to prevent first, and then cure disease. One well known medical professional who supports this approach is Dr. Deepak Chopra. Raised and trained in the medical field in India, he continued his studies in the United States and held prestigious medical positions in this country. He combines his Eastern and Western expertise in medicine in a very unique way. Books such as *Ageless Body, Timeless Mind* and the audio program *Perfect Health* provide essential information in the area of preventing illness and preserving wellness.

From a different perspective, spiritual and physical wellness has been the focus of teaching for the greatest spiritual masters on Earth. The four gospels of the New Testament contain the teachings of Christ on this theme. As we have seen, some of the original meaning of his teachings has been altered or lost over the centuries, eventually being transformed by the Church into an insensitive and rigid doctrine of fear. In the beginning, Christianity was Christ's religion, but soon became a religion about Christ. This is suggestively presented by The Teaching Company in 2004 in a course entitled *"From Jesus to Constantine: A History of Early Christianity,"* by Professor Bart D. Ehrman of The University of North Carolina at Chapel Hill. There are many researchers who suspect a much deeper substance in the words of Jesus.

During the first half of the 20th century, the controversial life of Jesus was uniquely analyzed by the so-called "Sleeping Prophet," Edgar Cayce. Originally a Bible teacher, Cayce accidentally discovered his ability to prescribe remedies for ill people, some even located in remote places such as South America. In a state of semi sleep he gave about 14,000 such "readings," which are presently well kept and organized at The Atlantic University, in Virginia Beach. My visit to this fascinating library in the summer of 1990 was one of the most enlightening experiences of my life. Many volumes have been written about his life and readings, but the most fascinating to me are those that discuss Cayce's contribution to the understanding of the origin of the human race and the true history of the Christian Church.

Especially when many reputable scientists maintain the same idea, their collective voice is strong enough to capture our attention. That is the case with one of the most fascinating collections of "mystical writings of the world's greatest physicists" entitled *Quantum Questions*, and edited by Ken Wilber. Here are the famous names, in the order Wilber's book presents some of their writings which I discussed and quoted in the chapter Scientists For Unity (I): Heisenberg, Schroedinger, Einstein, De Broglie, Jeans, Plank, Pauli, and Eddington. In the Preface of *Quantum Questions*, the editor summarizes very well the argument presented by all these physicists: "Modern physics offers no positive support (let alone proof) for a mystical world view. Nevertheless, every one of the physicists in this volume was a mystic." Since they all speak to the unity model of the universe, I consider their opinions to be solid support for the new paradigm I am proposing.

As we have already seen, Einstein is said to be one such "mystic." Not only was he one of the most influential physicists of the 20th century, but he also offered penetrating reflections on a large variety of other human concerns. Many volumes of Einstein's writings have been published in the United States as English translations from the German originals, including two exemplary works: *Ideas and Opinions* and *The World as I See It*. The scientist who gave us the Theory of Relativity had a lot to say on some of the issues considered in this book. Here are a few of Einstein's more significant essays: "Good and Evil," "The True Value of a Human Being," "Education and Educators," "Religion and Science," "Culture and Prosperity," "On Scientific Truth," "Education for Independent Thought," and "Ensuring the Future of Mankind."[68]

There have been many scientists who continued Einstein's work. Physicists are promoting now the unified field theory of the universe. Beside experiments, scientific articles, and books, video programs have been made available recently in an effort to express complex realities in common terms. I think three video programs are significant in this respect and I encourage the reader to watch them: *Mindwalk, What the (Bleep) Do We Know, and Down the Rabbit Hole*. They present an astonishing reality: we are all one, and we should be much better off by adopting this paradigm as our core existential conviction.

Also recently, the aforementioned trilogy *Conversations with God* by Neale Donald Walsch, which sold about 7 million hard copies in more than 30 languages, has been presented in large portions on audio tapes and it has helped change the way many people around the world see God. The story behind the trilogy is that of the author who had spent some time as a homeless person selling aluminum cans to survive. Later one night, at a low point in his life, he posed some very direct questions to God. To his fascination God was there: in his head the author received very clear and often unorthodox answers to some of the most ardent questions he asked. Starting in 1996 and over the next three years the question-answer sessions with God led to the known trilogy. Of course one can question the possibility for God to participate as a real conversational partner in this manner. Was it just a conversation anybody can have with their own conscious or subconscious mind? In this trilogy God suggests that we should think outside the box, to understand God as the universal intelligent and *omnipresent* energy. Consequently, such questions answer themselves: God *can* communicate in any possible way, not limited to one particular form or another as most major religions would like us to believe. An independently produced motion picture based on *Conversations with God* and the life of Neale Donald Walsch has been released in 2006. As expected, the universal union and interdependence of all that is in the universe is an important theme of the movie.

Chapter 11:

A New Paradigm for Modern Education

*Security can only be achieved through constant change,
through discarding old ideas that have outlived their use-
fulness and adopting others to current facts.*

William O. Douglas

An Overview

Since the education we receive directly affects the way we live, I would like to start this chapter by restating briefly what most philosophers and spiritual thinkers suggest that the real quality of life should be. Modern times, with so much emphasis on the material side of life, forced the human ego to high and dangerous levels of selfishness. A brief examination of the real fruits of such an existential philosophy reveals real human social conditions that are most unsatisfactory, characterized by high levels of crime and unhealthy habits. People inflict harm on people unconsciously, due to a lack of previous positive educational training, or consciously, due to a poor understanding of who we really are and our place in the universe. This is the direct result of the existing separation paradigm which suggests that harming others does nor directly harm ourselves. Consequently, the present belief must be drastically amended through a shift in our perception of who we really are and also regarding the real values we need to heed in our lives. As we have seen in previous chapters a majority of thinkers suggest that the real values are the perennial ones. These values do not depend on temporal material possessions or fleeting professional positions in our society. What we take with us to the next realm of existence at the time of death is not the money, the house, the car, or the high paying job we acquired during this lifetime. We will definitely take with us all that we have been giving away while here on Earth.[69]

The love we have given to others, the compassion, the understanding, the patience, and the respect we showed for other living forms
is what constitutes our real treasure. Eastern mysticism affirms
clearly that what is real is that which does not change. Indeed, all
material forms change, as opposed to the eternal positive energy
that is manifested through love, compassion, and patience. Consequently, the real values in life are nonmaterial and they are manifested through the vibrations of the most sensitive chords in
ourselves.

If the existing Western educational paradigm were an efficient
one, real human values would prevail in our society leaving no
room for crime and unhealthy practices. Especially today, when we
witness such rapid scientific and technological advances, we
should expect a parallel development in the most sensitive area of
human existence, namely the inner world. On the contrary, it seems
that this precise area is being heavily neglected, and the inevitable
lack of balance leads to many disasters. The separation paradigm,
based on the Greek scientific model of Aristotle and the rigid fundamentalist religious doctrine, allows people to inflict pain on others.

Such patterns of behavior are assimilated through general education within a paradigm of a presumed triple separation between
God, humans, and nature. The desire to eliminate negative acts and
worries from our society is the chief motivation for my attempt to
define a new educational paradigm of inclusion, union, love, and
compassion. I base this model on new and old evidence put forth
by thinkers in two major existential areas: science and spirituality.

Today, as never before, we may finally arrive to a clear understanding of our position in the world. Once we logically perceive
all forms of life (including ourselves) as implicit and vital components of a great organism called the cosmos, united through an infinite number of subtle levels of energy, we should realize that it
makes no sense for one human being to harm another. Furthermore, we should not harm other living forms or nature either. Here
is a parallel that can illustrate this very well: as it makes no logical
sense for my right hand to consciously inflict pain on my left leg,
it makes equally no sense for one human being to harm another.
The parallel is of course evident when we realize the connection

and mutual dependency between different organs, as human beings are "different organs" in the living organism we call the universe—the uni-verse.

Our aim should be to make this kind of awareness available to every single human being, so that we can ensure positive behavioral results all across the board. As the Western world is concerned, this knowledge can routinely be delivered through the variety of educational channels in place. Through books, audio and video tapes, radio and television, through media that have a strong hold on our attention, and through standardized academic education, the present view on life can be changed.

As it is obvious that the separation paradigm leads to human disasters, we should adopt the new model of union, compassion, understanding, patience, and love among all people. Racial discord is pointless when we see each other connected at the source of our existence. Crime motivated by unjust passion or desire for material possessions has no place when we realize the implicate order and balance described so eloquently by physicist David Bohm. Moreover, unhealthy rituals or habits should disappear when we understand the crucial points made by Matthew Fox and Rupert Sheldrake. Our efforts toward the implementation of the new paradigm should ensure that once a "critical number" of people practice good habits in the human morphic field, positive results will be imminent.

Let us examine now how such implementation can take place in important areas of our lives such as family, religious practice, the workplace, entertainment, and spiritual development.

Family Education

Most of us agree that a crucial role of the family is the education of children. Prior to their school years, children receive the core of human values in their families. Some statistics show that few children in the United States live in households with both biological parents present. Therefore, it seems essential that more children should be raised in complete families. The educational paradigm of union should build the necessary understanding of this need, such that both parents realize their responsibilities for the well-being of their children. Unjust selfishness has no place in the household, and as a positive result, more children should benefit from a complete family environment. This is in perfect accord with Rupert Sheldrake's morphic field theory, which states that, through morphic resonance, newly created educational habits will be learned much faster by other members of the respective species. Consequently, proper behavior by parents will be adopted by other parents faster than in the past, and similarly, children's positive development in one place will benefit others remotely. In fact I think Sheldrake's theory is also verified through the easiness with which today's children learn new tasks (sports, school games, computer games, and so on).

However, children are not the only ones receiving an education within the modern family. Parents, grandparents, and relatives are also being educated through family interactions. Therefore, all members of a family should be included in the circle of responsibilities for personal education in the new spirit, such that they will have a positive impact on overall family well-being. We need to remember that we teach by example. Einstein expressed this best when he said: "The only rational way of educating is to be an example—if one can't help it, a warning example."[70] In general, the way we conduct our own lives is reflected in our children's conduct as in a perfect mirror. One essential lesson we can teach children through our own example is that everything we are against weakens us, while everything we are for empowers us. For example, we shouldn't encourage a "war on drugs." Instead, we should be for pure and healthy living, which will obviously lead to the elimination of drugs through the awareness we make available in our society.

Regarding our youth, Dr. Wayne Dyer expresses this very well in his program entitled *What Do You Really Want For Your Children*. He suggests that we should guide and step aside, we should detach from the outcome, and we should avoid being overly possessive in our relationship with our children. He encourages firm rules, but he recommends that we should enforce them with love and care, nourishing a sense of responsibility in our children. Even from a very young age, we can cultivate a practical understanding of the universal connection. The air we breathe can serve as a basic starting point since, in fact, we are actually exchanging matter and energy with each other through breathing. Another way for children to learn to appreciate life early in their development is by socializing and engaging in a large variety of activities such as arts, sports, gardening, and taking care of pets. This type of practical experience should gradually build in children a natural sense of balance and respect for all forms of life on Earth.

Moreover, the new educational paradigm shows that, in a perfectly ordered universe, there is no real place for accidents and victims. Therefore, we should abolish self-pity altogether. We should cultivate the real values of life without stressing negative concepts that undermine self trust, self-reliance, and self-esteem in children. From an early age they can learn that it is possible and highly recommended to always tell the truth, and that as they don't want others to harm them, they should not harm anybody else in any way. Of course, being truthful goes hand in hand with love, compassion, patience, generosity, understanding, and forgiveness. Perseverance in teaching real human values within the union paradigm will lead eventually to a better quality of life and a clearer understanding of our purpose on Earth.

Religious Education

As we have seen earlier, the religious implication in modern education is still very powerful and it is not my intent to deny the good that the Christian Church has done and does in the world. However, since quantum theory proposes a new understanding of the universe, which is much in accord with ancient mystic traditions, we should reconsider Jesus' biblical teachings. The separation paradigm that is apparent in the Bible is not as strong as the Church would like us to believe. As we have seen earlier Jesus taught union, unconditional love and compassion in a harmony that was based on his conviction that God is in humans, humans are in Christ, and "me and my Father are one." In his mystic teachings we find ideas similar to scientific revelations of quantum physics, which makes us ask once again why are the 18 years of Jesus' life missing from the Bible. Regardless of the answer, we can redirect Christ's energy into a more positive and responsible path simply by underlining those of his teachings that are not blindly dogmatic.

Let us start with the very notion of praying. Through words and singing, a Christian expresses his or her concerns and wishes to a personal God. This kind of prayer by its very nature does not allow the person to listen to God, to relax and to quiet his or her mind in order to reach a higher level of awareness and inspiration. The well known French philosopher Blaise Pascal said that all troubles spring from our inability to sit quietly in a room alone. Along these lines another sensitive saying suggests that silence is the only voice of God. With such ideas in mind, the new paradigm for religious education should focus more on listening to God through quiet time in deep venerable meditation. This will allow the human being within us to tune into the morphic fields of inspirational divinity.

One other idea that clearly comes from Jesus' words, in spite of all the Church's efforts to suppress it, is karma. Jesus referred to it whenever he wanted to convey the message of people's responsibility for their actions, or to explain certain situations impossible to understand otherwise. David Bohm's theory of the implicate order provides us with a scientific perspective on the reality of the immutable law of cause and effect. This is also in complete accord with *Conversations with God*, where it is suggested that nothing in the material universe happens at random. In order for any event to take place, the parts involved are already in complete spiritual agreement with each other as to what is about to occur. This implies that at a deeper level all participants are aware of the law of cause and effect and they act accordingly. Indeed, in a universe where order prevails, every cause implies an effect, and consequently, every effect becomes a cause for a future effect. In other words, there cannot be an action without a reaction and every reaction becomes an action in itself.

The union paradigm I am proposing does include the concept of the implicate order, which is really inseparable from the reality of universal interconnection. Therefore, it strongly considers karma as a fundamental teaching component. We can see once more that Christianity at large should implement some changes in order to amend its credibility in the modern world. So long as the separation model persists in Christian philosophy, the new science will remain distant from its faithful population.

It is important to remember that the model of separation is still taught in theology, as Matthew Fox mentions. Therefore, if we expect a meaningful change in the religious picture of the West, we should encourage an amendment in the teaching of the Bible, and especially the New Testament, especially to theology students. Christ's mysticism should be taught along with all the brief references still present in the Bible that remind us clearly of older Eastern traditions. As a comparison between Western religion and Eastern spirituality, Dr. Dyer reminds us that a religious person believes in God, while a spiritual person knows God. Indeed, one cannot know God so long as God is assumed to exist as a personal entity somewhere else in the universe, completely separated from the human being. Moreover, the reason fundamentalist Christianity promotes a personal God is because it follows the human model, where, in order to live in the present society, we have been taught to see each other as separate personal entities with needs, responsibilities, and desires. Understanding God as the universal energy that permeates everything, there is no other personality which God can be related to, hence there is no possible way to consider God a personal God. In this respect, one can know God, once God is understood as omnipresent, that is, existing everywhere: in a flower, a bee, a dog, and of course, in humans (according to Aquinas). Such new light might bring more scientists and clergy together, in an honest and open effort to reform science and Christianity simultaneously.

With this said, Christianity should revisit the dogma on which its present negative reputation is built upon. To impose faith by fear of "eternal damnation" versus bliss, is far remote from any reasonable assumption. In light of the mystical and scientific evidence of universal balance and union presented in this book, to be condemned to eternal punishment for a mere lifetime of human deeds makes little sense. Therefore, if Christianity really aims to serve humankind, it should go back to its mystical roots of compassion, union, and unconditional love, within an understanding of God as a universal intelligent energy, omnipresent and timeless, and above all, a God without needs. By abolishing the creed that postulates an insecure personal God who is assumed to dictate by fear, punishment, and rewards (a God made by humans in their own image), the Church will be able to incorporate the present scientific facts in their teachings, transforming its content into a true and needed religion for the new millennium. Most religious parents and grandparents educate their youth based on their own spiritual and religious awareness. Therefore, the Church will do well to reeducate its older devotees under the union paradigm in order to register a positive impact on the future.

Workplace Education

One other major provider of education is the place of work. As employees, not only do we learn to perform our duties, but we learn to do it in the way that it has been done before, with often little or no personal power of decision. Most of the time innovations are met with heavy reservations. The working philosophical paradigm of the past, which evolved over centuries under the aforementioned scientific and religious model of separation, is being preserved. Work ethics are, therefore, subject to the same debate as the true essence of Christianity. A perfect example of such debate in the employment arena can be any scandal involving presidents of the United States (one can think of a few). After all allegations, personal claims of misconduct, and possible legal implications, it is evident that, regardless of the truth, some of the people involved in such scandals are actually lying about their acts. This means that their personal existential philosophy, based on the present model of separation, permitted lying in the hope that if nobody proved them wrong, their injustice shouldn't hurt. Being truthful is one of the fundamental values that people should treasure. This one ethical norm, if followed and respected unconditionally, especially within the parameters of professional employment, would eliminate a great deal of suffering for all of those involved. We must also remember that the Biblical Ten Commandments of the Old Testament include this value, and they do so without leaving any alternatives, options, or flexibility: people should not lie. I would like to add that an old Inca salute says this clearly: work hard, don't lie, and don't make anybody suffer. However, in spite of such teachings, the modern Western world pays little attention to this. Examples are abundant to precipitate deeper reflection regarding the need for a more complete implementation of the ethical norm of honesty.

Once we know who we are in the larger scheme of the universe, once we logically understand the union, interconnection, and interdependence of all things (including human beings), we are finally convinced to incorporate this vital ethical norm in the way we conduct our lives including at the workplace. Not only being thoughtful of others by keeping the promises we make, but also being true to ourselves should constitute traits of a dependable human being. As more and more of us consciously respect these principles and make them a permanent practice, the morphic resonance proposed by Dr. Sheldrake will facilitate its rapid adoption by a vast majority.

Since we spend a considerable amount of time at work, this should also be pleasant. In this respect it seems logical that everyone of us should find that line of work that brings most pleasure. It makes a huge difference to love what we do instead of just working to make a living. Moreover, it is much easier to incorporate the highest norms of behavior and responsibility once we know we want and we like what we do for a living. In this respect Kenneth Kraft puts it very well in his *The Wheel of Engaged Buddhism* when he says: "The foundation of practice on this path is to become one with your work, giving it your full energy and attention."

Consequently, with responsible employees the ethical level of our place of employment rises. In parallel, employers become more aware of the paramount importance of the education that takes place while people are engaged in productive endeavors. It is obvious that any worthwhile line of work such as car-makers, cooks, professional educators, doctors, politicians, police officers, and so on, is ultimately meant to serve humanity. With this understanding in mind, it becomes even more ironic that, while at the place of employment, deceit is even considered. Therefore, the new educational paradigm should shed clear light on the actual unity between human beings regardless of the distance that apparently separates them. In turn, this should contribute to the realization that one must act responsibly at all times, since the effects of each human action cannot be separated and it cannot be canceled in the universal connection and interdependence of all that is.

Entertainment Education

In the pursuit of relaxation and rest the human race has been very inventive over time. The modern era offers the most complex entertainment arsenal known to the historical development of humankind. However, the present separation paradigm has guided the entertainment industry on a money-making path that often ignores not only the very essence of a human being but also the human connection with and dependency on the environment. Slowly, the Westerner lost reverence for nature, for animals and plants, as biologist Rupert Sheldrake points out. As a result, we search for excitement in dangerous and often risky ways. Skydiving, parachute and bunjie jumping, all terrain motorcycle and car racing, and horror movies together with overly violent cartoons and computer games are only a few examples of such entertainment activities. These forms of entertainment are almost invariably paired with fear, risk, and a feeling of exhilaration that are meant to substitute for and surpass the pleasure, contentment, and excitement one experiences through generally risk free sports, safe hiking, traveling, reading, closer observation of nature, the traditional well organized Olympic kind of games, and so on.

In this age of electronic communication many such adventures are being made available to anyone with access to a cable television, and even more recently, to a computer with Internet connection. During countless hours of television watching and personal computer use, people are educated on the competitive and often selfish side of life. It is no surprise that Western society has developed an appetite for violent action movies and scenes of aggression in the daily news. This habit, repeated often enough, does seem to propagate itself faster as time allows more people to tune in to the morphic fields suggested by Dr. Sheldrake. Within the existing paradigm of human isolation in separated bodies that somehow learned how to think, the survivor's fight seems logical—very much like the survival in the wild.

However, the new educational paradigm, based on the universal union and interdependence of all that is, implies a radically different model for the whole entertainment industry. Once they realize the true nature of the world and our place in the larger scheme of things, those in charge of producing such programs will use their awareness to endorse a positive and responsible message. I believe that such a shift has already begun especially through some television channels that present sensitive programs meant to diminish the negative aspect of unnecessary violence.

Since the entertainment industry is a gigantic money-making endeavor, it will be difficult to change its existing focus from producing merely what sells, to a more noble aspiration such as producing what would be truly good for the human race in the long run. In order to overcome this obstacle, a shift in the specialized education of the professionals involved in this industry becomes imperative.

Finally, we arrive at the massive field of standard academic education that pretends to set the foundation for the teaching of practical moral and ethical human values. Offered through such a large variety of institutions, academic education can help shape human beings who will be capable of eradicating negativity and violence from their lives. This will not only reduce the number of customers applauding violent entertainment, but it will also assure positive future change in the way people spend their leisure time.

Spiritual Education

What the fundamentalist Christian religion teaches is that we live one life that is followed by *an eternity* in either heaven or hell. In accordance to the logical description of the purpose of life as presented in the aforementioned *Conversations with God*, *eternal* of anything makes no sense first, because independent time does not exist, and second, because God itself wanted to get out of conceptualized experience.

Instead, God wanted to *feel* what it means to live experiences in flesh and bones so to speak. It is much like the difference between watching a basketball game on television while not knowing anything about playing the game yourself. More realistic and fulfilling is stepping on the court, shooting baskets, dribbling, passing the ball to teammates, and most importantly, experiencing the feeling of winning or loosing an important game.

And this tells all: winning or loosing! The duality of the physical universe (dark-light, inside-outside, good-bad, positive-negative, cold-warm, etc.) was a must for what God intended to live by *experience*. As God puts it in *Conversations with God*, "in the absence of what you are not, that what you are is not." One cannot experience *good* without knowing *bad, inside* without *outside*, and so on. Therefore, when it comes to *eternity* in either heaven or hell, as Christianity presumes we will experience after death, there is a dilemma: it is not possible to *experience* only good (heaven) or only bad (hell) forever—after all, God was *only* good (love) before introducing the illusion of bad in order to create the duality necessary for physical experience. In reality one means nothing without the other. However, a word of warning is in order: we should not rush to say that *bad* is a necessity *in our world* and, therefore, we should tolerate it! In an infinite universe good and bad do not have to take place at the same physical location. God can *materialize* any experience of duality, including good and bad, in remote locations.

Therefore, we should go back to the words of Einstein who said that in order to survive and to teach true spirituality, Christianity should redefine itself and should rebuild a trust in the population of the modern world. This implies that the religious education in the Christian World should incorporate new elements or rediscover the lost teachings of Jesus. So much of Christ's teachings have been misinterpreted, or intentionally changed to fit a certain dogmatic doctrine of fear of punishment that the beautiful message of unconditional love, compassion, patience, and understanding has been lost.

Consequently, all Christian faiths should teach the union paradigm across the board, in order to connect the new with the old, the religious and spiritual with the scientific. Most importantly, they should connect what is theoretical with that which is practical. Moreover, the dogmatic teachings and the imposition of unquestionable doctrine should make room for analysis, for open dialogue, for debate, and finally, there should be room for change. This is so much more needed in modern times when we witness so many inhuman acts committed exactly by the clergy of different Christian denominations: pedophiles among Catholic priests, nun murdered in Romania in 2005 by Christian Orthodox monks, several Christian extreme sects such as the Branch Davidians from

Waco, Texas, etc. I cite here only a few cases (in fact they might represent only the tip of the iceberg) to prove that the traditional teachings are not convincing enough to help one actually live the high moral and ethical values. Thus, once again the need for the adoption of the union paradigm is evident.

Chapter 12:

The Future is Open

---

*Happy are those who dream dreams and are ready to pay
the price to make them come true.*

L. J. Cardinal Suenens

Personal Growth

It is universally accepted that the personal traits of a human being
are evident in all aspects of that person's life, or in other words,
who we are we take with us everywhere we go. Consequently, we
need to focus on the inner personal changes made possible by the
union paradigm. In spite of the fact that our five senses do not
allow us to perceive the universal union (after all we do not perceive radio and television waves either—and they are real), we are
all one, indeed. Through the realities of quantum physics the new
understanding of the world affects us deeply because it remind us
constantly that we are connected to all things, close or far.

By "all things" I mean every single material body, every
action, and every possible state of existence. Being connected
means that through our participation *we* are actually at the root
cause of all things "happening" to us. By assuming responsibility,
the concept of accidental events in our lives should be completely
eliminated. Therefore, we can release the blame we so often place
on circumstances or on other people, and, as the subtitle of this
book suggests, we can finally be free of all worries. From this perspective we can see an illness, for example, as a part of our cosmic
evolution. This realization will enable us to live through physical
pain with no suffering. Indeed, since suffering is the result of feeling victimized, within the union paradigm we can understand pain
as a necessary process chosen by ourselves for specific reasons at
a higher level of awareness.

Moreover, we should also consider pain from a non physical perspective. So many people suffer tremendous emotional and psychological pain that through hate can lead to crime. Here are some of such circumstances: divorce, jealousy, envy, fear, loss of a loved one, loss of money or property, loss of a job, the feeling of failure, the feeling of discrimination, the feeling of loneliness, the feeling of inferiority, and so on. All of these are feelings that spring from our perception of the world. Within the existing paradigm of separation all these feelings cause a lot of suffering in people since they see themselves victimized *from the outside*. As soon as we understand the union of all that is we can perceive emotional and psychological pain differently. Yes, we feel it, but we don't allow it to ruin our lives. Instead, we can use the pain we feel as a stepping-stone in our development, knowing full well that at a deeper level of awareness *we* attracted it into our lives. As we understand that the next person is connected to us within the making of our world, we will not even think of striking at them in any shape or form. Instead, we will do our best to help them realize that indeed we are all one and we should strive together for the betterment of all people.

With this philosophy as a guide, one of the greatest contributions we can make to our society is to teach our children to take responsibility for their thoughts and actions and also teach them to accept their pain, but not to subject themselves to suffering. Such teaching will eventually build future generations of "non blamers," responsible people who will live their lives at a higher level of awareness.

Academic Education

Relative to modern academic education let us return to Einstein's *Ideas and Opinions* where he says:

> I want to oppose the idea that the school has to teach directly that special knowledge and those accomplishments which one has to use later directly in life. The demands of life are much too manifold to let such a specialized training in school appear possible. Apart from

that, it seems to me, moreover, objectionable to treat the individual like a dead tool. The school should always have as its aim that the young man leave it as a harmonious personality, not as a specialist.[71]

As we examine the school systems of the West, we can readily notice that they basically teach the knowledge necessary for a certain diploma, hence for a certain job or field. Standards generally set in place within closed academic circles are declared to be sufficient. However, Einstein's "harmonious personality" is rarely found in today's graduates. The paradigm of union addresses this issue by encouraging a broad education which should include courses in general philosophy and meaningful, objective, applicable religion and spirituality, such that the graduate leaves school as a well rounded intellectual, versus a "dead tool."

If we are to implement such teaching in the scientific and technological areas, which are very popular today, educators should become open enough to include those components of modern science that speak to the new vision of the universe. Quantum revelations should be made available to students in all areas of study. I have been very impressed by many of my own students who displayed deep interest in such issues as the perfect order, the connection between all things, and even in discussion on the meaning of life. Therefore, it is my observation, which springs from 24 years of classroom experience, that students of all ages are really hungry for such "educational delicacies," as I call them. This kind of open discussion should be made available to all students in a non threatening way, such that they have an opportunity to approach subjects of existential concern in addition to the purpose of the course at hand. Not only will such conversation facilitate a more amicable relationship between teacher and student, but it will also serve as a counseling session within the standard realm of the curriculum. In fact, this is the subject of debate in a *United States News & World Report* article entitled "Algebra and Sympathy,"[72] and is presented with the suggestive subtitle "In a tough world, teachers increasingly offer some of both." The argument is really in favor of organized or instant counseling, pointing out substantial improvement in the students' academic, behavioral, and self-esteem development. Although its main thrust is pro-counseling, the article does present some opposing views, such as the concern expressed by some parents who think that a "focus on students' emotional development" can be "an intrusion in their domain."

However, from my own experience with this kind of free spirited discussion in the classroom, I can say that proper boundaries can be set in order to avoid any "intrusion." It seems that more and more school systems implement teacher-student counseling, although some teachers don't feel at ease with shifting from the pure teaching mode to the sensitive counseling position. With this in mind, I would like to suggest, also as an important component of the new educational paradigm, that teachers should educate themselves on counseling issues, since to be an effective teacher requires more than merely teaching the subject matter. The professional ability of an instructor to put the content of the respective course of study in the larger perspective of a rapidly changing world becomes a must. Moreover, as Einstein expressed it, we need to teach for life's many facets, which implicitly include those sensitive areas that in the separation model of teaching and learning belonged to counseling, but were not included in the actual academic teaching.

As I see it, educators who want to contribute fully to the development of their students have two major choices: to educate themselves on the complex demands of modern society, or to change careers completely. In this book I raise some very ardent questions about the outcomes of modern education under the existing paradigm of separation. The levels of crime, including suicide, self-inflicted harm through practice of unhealthy habits, and extreme violence in the entertainment industry are all alarming signs suggesting that something is wrong with the accepted model of general education. In this respect the teachers are ultimately responsible for the general outcome of teaching and learning. Not only the subject matter as it is taught in our classrooms but also our own existential philosophy, as teachers and human beings, are passed on to the next generation. The quality of life in the Western world cannot and will not change until a critical "mass" of individuals gain a more constructive and meaningful existential practical philosophy. The academic part of education in any society is the most powerful teaching and learning sector. That is even more a reason to affirm that the role of the teacher should expand. The teacher should be able to instantly become a counselor, or to assume even a parenting role for those students in desperate need.

Many students are not prepared emotionally for life. They are not presented with a clear answer to the most important question of all: Why are we here? Ironically, in an era when we should search for the reason behind the events around us, the meaning of our own life, is hardly touched in modern education. That is assumed to be the area of religion and spirituality, combined with natural philosophy. Somehow, most degree plans leave this out of the standard curriculum probably assuming that it will be taken care of by the church or personal self growth efforts, which for many individuals are really absent from their lives. Therefore, in order to give students the most powerful motivator of all, academic education should be delivered by educators who can provide meaningful answers to such deep questions. Through the scientific, spiritual, and philosophical evidence presented in this book, the union paradigm can fill this gap. As an integral component of the world, the human race, through its awareness, sensitivity, and creativity is the conscious moving principle that can accomplish a rational understanding of all things. The omnipresent energy that holds the cosmos together is the force called by many names—from Brahman and Allah, to God and "the God particle." Not only is this energy omnipresent but it is also eternal; all that changes is its form, as water can change from solid ice to vapors. Therefore, since the human race has this energy within itself, it is eternal; all that changes is its form but not its spiritual essence. This essence exists forever, and we can adopt the age-old mystical understanding, also supported by many modern scientists, that the purpose of our material existence, hence our life, is to become aware of the higher universal order of which we are an inseparable part: we are all one. Of course, with such an understanding comes an unconditional responsibility: we should all strive to do good, positive, constructive, creative, compassionate deeds, and we should all be loving in all our endeavors.

To teach this understanding is another major component of the new educational paradigm. Although I have attended many professional conferences on modern education, I have yet to find presentations on themes such as "Love and Compassion in Teaching" or "Teaching the Meaning of Life," other than my own. Most professional efforts out there are on strategies for better retention, the use of technology, and helping students "at risk," with a special focus on minorities. The new paradigm is not at all meant to eliminate any of these important themes, but in order to make the existing efforts for better education truly fruitful, we need to dig deeper into the meaning of life, to research it, to teach it, and to make it understandable to students of all disciplines. Once we see our real place in the world and the universal union between all that is, we become aware and responsible for everything we think, say, or do. This kind of practical awareness will finally "take a bite out of crime," and in the end eliminate it completely.

Education and Technology

Such a high educational goal can be accomplished through a variety of means. However, the new trends in modern education are focused almost completely on the use of the latest technology. But although it often appears as a fascinating new tool, technology can be very deceiving. It is important to remember the loss of privacy and stolen identities facilitated by the "information super highway," and the real danger of "computer wars," since the same technology is also in the hands of criminal "cyber warriors."[73] It is a well known fact, also maintained by experts, that the United States is extremely vulnerable to a cyber attack. This is true indeed, since all vital functions of American society, such as transportation, energy, finance, and defense are totally dependent on information systems linked via numerous computers to the Internet. International groups have stated that the Internet is a weapon to be mastered against the United States (in 1994 a hacker broke through the United States military computer security and gained access to important defense information).

Virtual reality offered by the most advanced computer technology, on which much high-tech teaching is based, replaces real experience, even when used in technical areas of study. This becomes crucial in more sensitive teaching fields, such as nursing, where the direct human contact is vital for a clear understanding of the procedures involved in a successful job performance.[74] So long as we are facing an electronic screen, we cannot look people in the eyes. Consequently, the enormous amount of time we are forced to spend in front of a computer or television screen each day dictates the amount and the quality time we have left to spend with other human beings, especially with those from our immediate family. Although we can learn on the screen, excessive "screen watching" is in fact a modern addiction, a new malady of our time, and it is as detrimental to our mind, body, and soul as is any other dependency. Under the spell of a life in the fast lane through technology Western civilization teaches us that faster is better, and the sole motivator for such a belief is quick material gain. Although I understand the need for money, in many cases, money has made us forget our very nature, namely that we are human beings completely dependent on our surroundings, hence on nature and the environment. In the fast pursuit of money we forget to stop and admire the beauty around us. High-level technology pushed to extreme encourages unhealthy behaviors by promoting a fast approach in almost all areas of life. Unless we strike a balance at a personal level, this situation implicitly leads to impatience and short tempers as we chase fast food, fast entertainment, fast transportation, fast communication, and fast education.

A major warning sign regarding the downside of a "faster is better" philosophy is the loss of patience in human beings, which I mentioned before. As a result, we are overwhelmed by the high rate of divorce, by the incredibly high number of court cases, and by the general tendency of people to withdraw in isolation and avoid the responsibility involved in interacting with others. In academic education a good example of technological separation between human beings is a computer lab, as useful as it may be in some areas. In any modern school the following picture presents itself: lonely people sitting in front of impersonal computer screens, separated from their fellow human beings in the name of an education delivered exclusively by high-tech means. The reality is that the human aspect—the eye-to-eye contact, sensitivity, patience, and the element of human care—is being lost. As we examine these implications from a medical perspective, we shouldn't be surprised by the high rate of heart disease, drinking problems, smoking, drug abuse, obesity, high stress, and of course, the increasing rate of people suffering from terminal illnesses such as cancer. Implicitly, these are also some of the results of the existing paradigm of separation.

As a constructive solution, the union paradigm I propose suggests a well balanced use of technology in education, in an effort to preserve as much human contact as possible between teacher and student. Moreover, under the new model, in order to ensure a healthy level of human contact, we should all slow down and "smell the roses," as the saying goes. New medical studies maintain, based on hard evidence, that the interconnection between mind and body is a fact (era two medicine).

Health Education

This revelation is another important part of the new educational model, and we should remember the well known Biblical advice: as you think so shall you be. Modern medical researchers, such as Dr. Larry Dossey and Dr. Deepak Chopra, have made available entire studies on subjects relating to the connection between mind, body, and soul.[75] One of these ideas, verified through successful experiments, is that the mind does affect the body (the placebo effect and meditation), and moreover, the mind can affect the body of someone else, at a remote location, hence the non local nature of the universe. I would like to mention here again the fascinating story of the "Sleeping Prophet," Edgar Cayce, who, for several decades during the first half of the 20th century, offered 14,000 accurate "readings" in the form of medical diagnoses and answers to a broad range of questions. Although they are apparently kept out of the mainstream of modern medical science, such studies allow us to reflect on real meaningful existential issues related to the unity model, which in turn ignite our desire for a better understanding of the beautiful world we live in.

As with any other effort to optimize human relationships, patience also requires training. However, patience training implies that we work on our skills, which necessarily consists of improvement on the use of our sense of perception. Becoming aware of the universal union we will show unconditional respect and consideration for other human beings. Through this kind of education, the "victim" syndrome will vanish. Consequently, the new educational paradigm should incorporate live sessions of human interaction in all academic settings: teachers and students, students among themselves, and teachers with teachers.

Since I consider academic education (or the lack of it) responsible for many other socially harmful practices, I would like to show how the union paradigm can improve our lives. It can be argued that human rebellion, for example, which often leads to personal or social disasters, has its roots in the individual's or group's insecurity. Many people rebel when they feel threatened by the social establishment, or by individuals in power. For example, gangs form and riots erupt in order to show disobedience to perceived unfair laws, or simply to manifest disagreement with decision making authorities. The chief motive for this kind of unhealthy behavior is a deep insecurity that springs from a misunderstanding of who we are, why we are here, and where we are heading as human beings. I assert that the separation model in the modern world trains us to see people in a continuous struggle against each other, as every individual attempts to defend a set of ideas that describes his or her priorities in life. As we saw earlier, this existential philosophy has been encouraged by a system of academic education based on a 2,000-year old picture of the world, which was set in place and supported by Greek science and philosophy combined with dogma promoted by organized religion. However, in light of all the evidence accumulated in this book the new educational model is capable of presenting a more realistic makeup of our world. People are connected, we are all different organic parts of a complex body, and at a subtle energetic level, we are all one, regardless of skin color, ethnicity, gender, sex orientation, or religious belief. Since our limited five senses are not able to provide a clear perception of such reality, we should rely on the wisdom of modern science, mysticism, and ancient spirituality. With such information at hand one can build a natural existential philosophy that is not only positive, peaceful, and constructive, but also capable of providing enough common sense reasons to deter any kind of rebellious violent acts against individuals or the entire society. The new educational paradigm, made available through academic institutions and from person to person, should be able to eliminate any trace of individual and group insecurity. Living with the conviction that, within the unity of all things, by harming others we actually harm ourselves, we should finally let go of the dangerous desire to always be right. Instead, we should choose to be kind, as Dr. Wayne Dyer suggests so eloquently.

As far as the world-wide education is concerned Albert Einstein maintains that since traditions and customs are different from place to place we should always strive for the constructive ones. Consequently, the largely harmful separation paradigm we have in place in our system of education today should be replaced by the more promising model of union I propose. I will end this chapter with Einstein's words:

It certainly makes more sense to ask which institutions and traditions are harmful, and which are useful, to human beings; which make life happier, or more painful. We then must endeavor to adopt whatever appears best, irrespective of whether, at present, we find it realized at home or some-where else.[76]

Chapter 13:

What it All Means

Teach this. Teach this. All else will fall into place.
Here are four words to memorize:
We are all one.
Model that when you make your next choices
and decisions.

Tomorrow's God: Our Greatest SpiritualChallenge,
By Neale Donald Walsch, author of *Conversations with God.*

In Brief

I would like to summarize the impressive volume of evidence pertaining to the common ground of science, religion, and spirituality, which speaks to the core of the union paradigm I am proposing. From actual statistics and real facts of life that characterize modern society, to philosophical and scientific opinions of consecrated contemporary professionals in science and religion, we are faced with a picture of human behavior that desperately needs improvement. Most of the evidence made available by so many positive thinkers, contributes to the design of the new model. Especially the obvious parallel between quantum physics and ancient Eastern spirituality, is capable of bringing some sense of unity among areas thought of as separated in the past. Moreover, the morphic fields theory advanced by Rupert Sheldrake is meant to show that all species are actually connected through an invisible web of information, and that we should be more responsible in anything we think and do because we all are, indeed, implicit components of the universal organism, and we are, at a deeper energy level, dependent on each other.

From a spiritual point of view the evidence included here presents the key elements of a religion stripped of dogmatic teachings. Matthew Fox contributes clearly to the clarification of such issues as he underlines the mysticism of Christ that is not openly accepted by the Church, and its role in constructing a more accurate picture of our universe. Hand in hand with the ancient Eastern mysticism, through the teachings of Jesus, Christianity does include many elements that add substantially to the formation of the union paradigm I am proposing.

One remarkable personality with clear positive views was, of course, Albert Einstein. I included in here several suggestive quotes from some of his memorable reflections on education, religion and science, teachers and students, and on our future. Einstein belongs to an elite of scientists who had meaningful things to say about the nature of the universe from a scientific point of view. Although some contradictions do appear in the views of modern scientists, they seem to be more of a superficial nature than of substance.

Sciences such as quantum physics, biology, and mathematics have been the focus of much of my book's findings. The evident parallel between quantum mechanics and Eastern mysticism described so eloquently by Fritjof Capra in *The Tao of Physics*, stands as a building block in the wall of the new paradigm of union.

As a personal support for the unity paradigm I included some of my own experiences, many of which led to my research for this book. I hope they will help you, the reader, to refine your understanding of the new philosophy and eventually to teach it to others.

Finally, in the chapter entitled "A New Paradigm for Modern Education" I presented several areas of life where the new ideas can be incorporated. Because general education is facilitated by such a variety of human endeavors, my intention was to present the key elements of the new educational model as they apply to those specific areas. The actual implementation of these ideas can vary from case to case, depending on the situation and the background of the people involved.

However, the results should all be positive. In a united world there is no more room for senseless discords, and under the new paradigm such a world *is* possible. The quantum union of all that is, viewed from the material perspective as well as through the ancient spiritual traditions, should become common sense for each human being in the world.

Conclusions and Implications

In previous chapters I presented the main motivation for this book. I underlined the fact that our society displays too much violence, negativity, and disregard for nature, and too little love, compassion, understanding, and patience. If the existing educational paradigm in the West were a successful one, the negative outcomes would be foreign to us. However, that is not the case. Therefore, the educational model, the general existential philosophy must be amended in order to improve the outcomes, hence, the quality of our lives. The aim of this work is two-fold. On one hand it illustrates how the existing paradigm of separation between man, God, and nature has created an existential and educational philosophy which fails to provide all human beings with the necessary logical understanding of the need for high moral and ethical standards in the society. On the other hand it proposes a new educational paradigm within the understanding of the universal union and interconnectedness of all that is, based on scientific evidence and spiritual reasoning.

Throughout this book I presented an ample volume of documentation in support of the union paradigm. The existing research is abundant and it is made available to everyone through many channels such as books, audio tapes, CDs, videotapes, DVDs, specialized television channels, and public meetings and conferences.

A presentation of some of the problems existing in the Western world was followed by a discussion of different educational channels available in our society. The definite role of Christianity, as the major religion of the West, is presented from two perspectives. One such view is based on the role it played over centuries as a promoter of the separation paradigm, while the other presents Christianity as a potential teacher of unity and unconditional love through the truly mystical teachings of Jesus. Since the metaphysics of his teachings goes hand in hand with the older Eastern spirituality, and since this spirituality postulates facts which are being verified by modern science, the rest of the book takes us towards the formulation of the educational paradigm of union by connecting science, religion, and spirituality.

Although it is not necessarily a simple endeavor to amend an old and well established model of thinking, it is possible that gradual implementation of the main points presented in the new paradigm, could change the general human behavior for the better one person at a time. Gandhi expressed this very suggestively: we need to become the changes we want to see in the world. Along this line, awareness of the implicate order in the universe and realization of the subtle union of all that is, might provide us with enough common sense reasons for a positive shift in our perception of life, and therefore, a change in our attitude towards fellow human beings. This can solve all major modern problems that translate in human worries, some of which are: racism, gender discrimination, child and spouse abuse, religious discrimination, environmental concerns, senseless political competition, fear of sickness and death, international conflict, and so on. Also the victim syndrome will vanish with the understanding that nothing happens accidentally in a perfectly balanced universe where, in fact, we are the creators of our own reality. This paradigm change implicitly takes us to "the end of all worries."

To make it all possible, we should strive to gain the personal responsibility necessary to enroll on such an important mission of change. The general academic education system is the main avenue for such a revolutionary shift. In order to bring higher awareness to as many people as possible, professionals in all educational areas should consider adopting the new and more constructive understanding of the universe presented here. After the assimilation at the professional level of the educators, the new paradigm should be incorporated in the teaching of every academic subject from kindergarten through doctoral programs. This will ensure that the parents of tomorrow will teach their own children the existential philosophy that says "We Are All One," based on the appreciation of pure truth and respect for all life forms. Unconditional love for all human beings should be a given once we all understand that people are on their own individualized planes of existence which justifies their reaction to the world around them. As Dr. Hagelin maintains, this kind of understanding can be achieved also through the practice of meditation. This is a very well documented way to expand one's perception of the world, although "It's the world's best kept secret of actual power that each individual holds," says Hagelin.

Of course, the efforts toward positive solutions for the acute problems facing our modern society do not stop here. Further research is definitely needed in such a sensitive area as the human development. With this in mind, I am aware that the parallels between modern science, religion, and spirituality are very suitable for further investigation, and that is why I repeatedly made reference to other studies. Considering the actual implementation of the union paradigm in our lives, there is an imperious need for more practical ideas and suggestions. That is why I included some of my personal experiences that support the core of the union paradigm and I want to encourage you, the reader, to search for your own. My hope is that the critical number of supporters and practitioners of the union paradigm will be reached soon, so that the morphic field theory proposed by Dr. Sheldrake will make this knowledge instantly available to the rest of the world.

Financial Implications

The financial implications of the unity paradigm are three-fold. First, individuals will benefit from saving the money spent to protect themselves against crimes that are not going to take place when all humans understand the universal connection and interdependence. Second, local city and state management will be able to allocate the money spent on crime related issues—prosecution, jails, prisons, endless expensive court hours, racism associated conflicts, domestic disputes—on more needed areas such as education, care for the elderly, medicine, preservation of the environment, scientific research, and so on. Third, nations will be able to use most of the funds they presently allocate to armament to many constructive domestic endeavors.

In this respect, we also need to think of the long term worldwide implication of the new paradigm in preventing a much anticipated third world war. As we look around the world we can locate multiple possible centers for the start of a planetary conflict. From the Middle East and Africa, to the Korean peninsula, one can only anticipate an explosion of international insecurity that can engage the world in a devastating Armageddon. The message of unity that springs from this book and many other sources should finally arrive to governments all around the world. If nations become aware of the implicit union of all that is on Earth—remember Dr. Edgar Mitchell's revelation on the Moon—there will be a good chance to prevent a global catastrophe.

If it will unfortunately materialize, such a somber event will most likely result from political and religious international discord which, as we have seen earlier, go hand in hand. Consequently, we will have to agree that just by understanding God differently from nation to nation, can destroy the very kingdom that presumably God intended on Earth. Outrageous sectarian violence such as the one we witness in Iraq proves this point. To the rescue, this book offers plenty of arguments to convince those who entertain dangerous ideas, to abolish them all together. Within a sense of personal and national responsibility, they should realize that there is no higher aspiration for a human being than to help other humans prosper. The reality of the paradigm of unity should convince each of us that by helping others we actually help ourselves. The financial gain resulting from such a change in behavior is once again obvious.

Political Implications

One well known comedian put it very well by saying that no human being living in the United States could define herself or himself as a Republican or a Democrat only: we are Republicans on some issues and Democrats on some other. I think there is a great deal of truth to this especially when we view it through the union paradigm. Once we realize that in fact *we are all one* in mind, body, and spirit, differences between Republican, Democrat, Independent, and even Natural Law Party fade, leaving room for the universal understanding that we are here all together, living under the same roof, so to speak. There will be no reason for continued discord and no more senseless and expensive political confrontation. Instead, there will be time, energy, and financial support available for mutual agreement and understanding, without necessarily abolishing political affiliation.

Celebration of Life

In the end that is all there is: Life. We can witness it everywhere, in humans, in animals, in plants, and even in the so called "non living matter." The minerals themselves display a type of living that escapes our day-by-day scrutiny (life of crystals, for example). The very omnipresence of God, or the universal intelligence, demonstrates that there is some form of life *everywhere* we look. Quantum physics confirms what Eastern spirituality and world-wide mysticism postulated for millennia. On the infinite scale of organized intelligence there is a place for every kind of *being*, let that be mineral, plant, animal, human, or superhuman.

With this image in mind we arrive to a point where we cannot but reconsider our perception of life: everything is living, everything is sacred, we are part of everything, everything affects us directly or indirectly and we affect everything. There is no more room for blaming the circumstances for our shortcomings. Instead, we should smile, understanding that at a deeper level of reality *we* selected them for our own progress through the complex web of universal consciousness.

In this respect, our relationship with immediate family members, with relatives, with neighbors, and even strangers takes a completely new meaning. A deep sense of peace will embrace every encounter. The need to prove one wrong will vanish, since we will understand that nobody is wrong given *their* model of the world, as it is so clearly presented in *Conversations with God*.

Another fundamental message from the same trilogy is that we should understand God as Life, using the word God and Life interchangeably. Moreover, we, as human beings, *are* an intrinsic part of life. This not only confirms our participation in the whole of creation but also implies that we should approach nature and the environment with respect and understanding, as we approach any other form of life. Storms and "bad weather" are as much part of the larger picture as everything else, including sunshine, and cool mornings. Therefore, the anxiety created by our way of thinking about "bad" circumstances will vanish along with all other related worries.

This change in philosophy will have such a remarkable effect on our well-being that we will never go back to the separation model. In the pursuit of true happiness, we will finally be able to love each other unconditionally and we will appreciate our natural environment to its real and vital value. The smell of a flower or the admiration of wildlife will awaken within us the feeling of oneness that we waited for so long. Under all the considerations presented in this book, *the wait is over!* We are finally ready to understand life, and therefore, God, as a unity from which we are an interdependent part. Within this understanding, we should celebrate life at every corner, and we should be ready to take conscious part in the process of constant recreation of our universe for a better tomorrow.

Chapter 14:

Presidents, Religious Leaders, and Terrorists!

Our children may learn about heroes of the past. Our task is to make ourselves architects of the future.

Jomo Kenyatta, first president of Kenya

I would like to bring the message of this book even closer to today's events of worldwide significance by addressing the human beings who, for best or for worst, intentionally or unintentionally, shape the present and the future of our planet. I am referring to presidents (government representatives) of all nations, religious leaders, and also to the leaders of the most notorious terrorist organizations in the world.

Human life on Earth displays natural tendencies toward union. The family, the neighborhood, the community, schools, business associations, sports teams, churches, labor unions, political parties, the states of a *union* (United Nations, United States of America, European Union), and so on, all represent the instinctive human need *to feel united*, to feel that people belong together to a larger order. This aspiration is only a reflection of the *universal union* that in fact holds the entire universe together. The reality of discord, of senseless competition, of terrorism, and of bloody wars, illustrates the primitive human animal instinct of *survival of the fittest*, which is wide spread in nature. In the meantime, this is still done in the name of some form of partial union: *us versus them*. Regardless of appearance, we *are all one*, united at the core of our existence. Only failure to realize this can set human beings against human beings.

When Edgar Mitchell (the sixth person to walk on the Moon) had his revelation of universal order, union, and interconnection described in this book, his view was not conditioned by anything; it was just the way it was. Sectarian religion, politics, ethnicity, race, skin color, gender, age, and sexual orientation were not factors in this realization. Our planet, the "blue quarter," incorporates all of it, indiscriminately: the past, the present, the good, the bad, the rich, the poor, the healthy, and the sick. It is, therefore, imperious for each of us, to realize that to be human means first of all to feel as one cell in the body of humanity. If for whatever reason a cell is acting against the well-being of the body, the nature of that cell needs to be changed. In fact that is how modern medicine assures a normal functioning of the human body. In this respect we know that in a majority of cases each individual human body tries instinctively to cure itself. If that is not successful, it is all left to others to intervene. Similarly, those who nurture thoughts of pointless aggression, cruel revenge, or domination, should become aware of the universal union, and they should try their best to change. The alternative will be for the rest of the human race to change them.

As far as *your* role as government representatives, religious leaders, and/or terrorists is concerned, it is obvious that *you* are on a position of solving much of the acute problem of worldwide hate. Based on the evidence cited in this book and various other scientific and spiritual testimonies, you can reexamine your understanding of the place we hold on our planet. Indeed, perceiving all people as interdependent and interconnected beings within the closed environment called Earth, there will be no more room for harming others. No political or economical reason will overtake this understanding. No interpretation of God as a revengeful, mean, and exclusive deity will be possible when we realize that if there is a universal God, there must be *only* one, no different for Christians, Jews, Muslims, or Buddhists. This God will not take sides. No twisting of spiritual scriptures will justify the killing of other human beings anymore. A God who allows lying and killing as long as it seems to serve a certain religious interpretation is not the universal and omnipresent God we should all cherish. The real omnipresent and omniscient God (or universal intelligence) will never encourage humans to fight humans, since that really means for God to fight God. In other words, what intelligence will fight against itself? The understanding of the physical subatomic and the spiritual connection of all that is in the universe sets the foundation for unity and the true long lasting peace and prosperity we all long for.

Presidents, religious leaders, and terrorists, at a personal level we can all implement the norms of the union paradigm, and our lives will instantly improve. However, because of the responsibility you have been given by the society or the role you have willingly taken upon yourselves, you are on a position to change the entire world. You can transform our planet from a place of senseless competition, domination, and discord, into a place of love, peace, compassion, freedom, cooperation, and prosperity for all nations. Under your leadership we can end hunger, racism, sexual abuse, political and religious fanaticism tomorrow. I hope you will join hands to reach this noble goal through open, honest, and positive negotiation.

In this respect I suggest that United Nations should organize yearly a "World Unity Summit for Heads of States" with the purpose of discussing the unity of all things and the immediate solutions that spring from the new paradigm. Quantum physicists and spiritual leaders should be invited to speak to you in light of the latest research on this matter. Be assured that the entire human race will be grateful for your efforts.

*

With this in mind, I want to encourage all readers to take action. There are many things you can do. Write to or talk to your local school, church, and government representatives and recommend this book and other sources of information on these lines to everybody. Share your ideas on union with relatives, friends, and neighbors. Pay closer attention to your own experiences and add to the already impressive volume of information on this important theme.

Together we can make a difference in the world as we depart from the paradigm of separation to embrace the true reality of universal union and interconnection. Knowing that WE ARE ALL ONE we can finally arrive to the actual *end of all worries* and take our true place in the universal scheme, which is that of indispensable participators and choice makers for the betterment of the human race.

I wish you well!

BIBLIOGRAPHY

Augros, Robert M. and George N. Stanciu.
  The New Story of Science, Bantam Books, 1984.

Blanchette, Oliva.
  The Perfection of The Universe According to Aquinas,
  The Pennsylvania State University Press, 1992.

Bloodworth, Venice.
  Key to Your-Self, DeVorss & Company Publishing, 1952.

Bock, Janet.
  The Jesus Mystery, Aura Books, Los Angeles, 1980.

Campbell, Joseph.
  The Power of Myth, Doubleday, New York, 1988.

Capra, Fritjof.
  The Tao of Physics, Shambhala, 1991.

Chopra, Deepak.
  Explorations Into Consciousness, Mystic Fire Video, Video
  tape.
  Ageless Body, Timeless Mind, Harmony Books.
  The Seven Spiritual Laws of Success, Mystic Fire Video,
  Video tape.
  Quantum Healing, Harmony Books.

Cook, John.
  The Book of Positive Quotations, Gramercy Books, 1993.

Dossey, Larry.
  Science, Spirit, & Soul, Sounds True, Audio tape.

Dyer, Wayne W.
　　A Promise Is a Promise, Hay House, Inc.
　　What Do You Really Want for Your Children, Avon Books.
　　The Secrets to Manifesting Your Destiny, Nightingale Conant,
　　Audio tapes.
　　Applying the Wisdom of the Ages, Nightingale Conant,
　　Audio tapes.

Dyer, Wayne W. & Deepak Chopra.
　　Living Beyond Miracles, New World Library, Audio tapes.
　　Creating Your World the Way You Really Want It to Be, Hay
　　House, Inc., Audio tapes.

Einstein, Albert.
　　Science and Religion, Crown Publishers.
　　Ideas and Opinions, Wings Books, 1954.

Ehrman, Bart D., Ph. D..
　　The History of the Bible: The Making of the New Testament
　　Canon, The Teaching Company, 2005.

Fox, Matthew.
　　The Coming of the Cosmic Christ, Harper & Row Publishers,
　　1988.

Fox, Matthew and Rupert Sheldrake.
　　The Sacred Universe, Sounds True, Audio tapes, 1993.

Fromm, Erich.
　　The Art of Loving, Harper & Brothers Publishers, 1956.

Head, Joseph and S. L. Cranston.
　　Reincarnation, An East-West Anthology, Aeon Publishing
　　Company, 2000.

Holy Bible.
　　Original King James Version, Dugan Publishers, Inc.,
　　Gordonsville, Tennessee 38563, 1987.

Lederman, Leon.
The God Particle, Houghton Mifflin Company, 1993.

Leek, Sybil.
Reincarnation: The Second Chance, Bantam Books, Inc., 1975.

MacLaine, Shirley.
Out on a Limb, Bantam Books.
Dancing in the Light, Bantam Books.
It's All in the Playing, Bantam Books.
Going Within, Bantam Books.

Murphy, Michael.
The Future of the Body, Putnam Publishing Group, 1993.

Prabhavananda, Swami.
The Spiritual Heritage of India, Vedanta Press, 1963.

Ram Dass.
Be Here Now, Crown Publishing.

Ram Dass & Mirabai Bush.
Compassion in Action, The Publishing Mills.

Rochlin, Gene I..
Trapped in the Net, Princeton University Press, 1997.

Rucker, Rudy.
Infinity and the Mind, Bantam Books, Inc., 1983.

Sheldrake, Rupert.
The Rebirth of Nature, Bantam Books, Inc., 1991.

Shenk, David.
Data Smog, HarperCollins Publishers, 1997.

Szekely, Edmond Bordeaux.
  The Essene Origins of Christianity, International Biogenic
  Society, 1993.

Sommer, Bobbe.
  Psycho-Cybernetics, 2000, Prentice Hall, 1993.

Talbot, Michael.
  The Holographic Universe, Harper Collins Publishers.
  Beyond the Quantum, Bantam Books.

The Holy Bible, Authorized King James Version, The World
  Publishing Company.

The Lost Books of the Bible, Gramercy Books.

The Oxford Companion to the Bible, Oxford University Press,
  1993.

Zukarov, Gary.
  The Dancing Wu Li Masters, Bantam Books, 1979.

Walsch, Neale Donald.
  Conversations with God—an uncommon dialogue—
  Books 1, 2, 3, Hampton Roads Publishing Company, Inc.,
  1996, 1997, 1998.

Walsch, Neale Donald.
  Tomorrow's God: Our Greatest Spiritual Challenge,
  ATRIA Books, 2004.

Wilber, Ken.
  Quantum Questions, Shambhala, 1985.

Woodward, Mary Ann.
  Edgar Cayce's Story of Karma, Berkley Books, 1980.

Notes:

1 Description presented by Fritjof Capra in *The Tao of Physics*.

2 *The Tao of Physics*, p. 22.

3 1 Corinthians 13:1,2,3,4,5,6,7.

4 Thomas Moore in *The Art of Simplicity*.

5 "the Nevada of South Asia" as it is described in the article.

6 From *Reincarnation, The second chance*, by Sybill Leek.

7 In spite of these efforts, Eastern spiritual teachings still remain in the Bible.

8 From *The Oxford Companion to the Bible*.

9 Matthew 4:17 and Mark 1:15.

10 "Adam which was *the son* of God", (Luke 3:38); "I ascend unto my Father, and your Father", (John 20:17).

11 Matthew 17:11,12,13; 19:17; Mark 8:27,28; Luke 1:17; John 3:3, 3:7.

12 Matthew 5:17; 5:39; 5:40;6:12; 7:12; Luke 6:31; 12:59; 18:14.

13 Matthew 5:48.

14 Dr. Bordeaux received a Ph. D. from the University of Paris, and other degrees from the Universities of Vienna and Leipzig. He was a professor of Philosophy and Experimental Psychology at the University of Cluj, Romania; versed in Sanskrit, Aramaic, Greek, and Latin, he also spoke 10 modern languages. Dr. Bordeaux translated selected texts from

the Dead Sea Scrolls, the Essene Gospel of Peace, and his work on the Essene Way of Biogenic Living became known worldwide.

15 From *The Essene Origins of Christianity*, by Dr. Edmond Bordeaux Szekely, p. 85.

16 See the Inquisition and even the involvement of the Vatican as partner with the Nazis in the Second World War ("A Vow of Silence," March 30, 1998 edition of United States News and World Report).

17 See the Jonestown, Waco, and other incidents of the 1980's and 1990's.

18 From *Key to Your-Self*, p. 65.

19 From *Key to Your-Self*, p. 64.

20 The quote I included here is my transcript from the original audio recording.

21 The Buddhist and Hindu traditions of the Far East.

22 *Out on a Limb*, Shirley MacLaine's autobiographical motion picture is also available.

23 New York: Harper and Row, 1971.

24 New York: Harper and Row, 1974.

25 New York: Harcourt and Brace, 1955.

26 *Quantum Questions*, p. 43.

27 *Quantum Questions*, p. 44.

28 Cambridge University Press ["C.U.P."], 1964.

29 C.U.P., 1958.

30 C.U.P., 1954.

31 C.U.P., 1951.

32 C.U.P., 1947.

33 *Quantum Questions*, p. 81.

34 *Quantum Questions*, p. 82.

35 *Quantum Questions*, p. 96‾97

36 Vedanta.

37 *Quantum Questions*, p. 97.

38 *Quantum Questions*, p. 97.

39 New York: Pantheon, 1955.

40 Quotes from *"The Two Sources of Morality and Religion"*.

41 From *Physics and Microphysics,* New York: Pantheon, 1955.

42 Cambridge University press, 1931.

43 *Quantum Questions*, p. 144.

44 *Quantum Questions*, p. 153.

45 *Quantum Questions*, p. 160.

46 *Quantum Questions*, p. 167.

47 *Quantum Questions*, p. 194.

48 *Quantum Questions*, p. 201.

49 *Quantum Questions*, p. 206.

50 *Ideas and Opinions*, p. 49.

51 *Ideas and Opinions*, p. 48.

52 Later, he stated that the detailed professional preparation for the space mission did not attempt to enhance astronauts readiness for such revelations; instead, they were heavily prepared technologically, conformed to the existing scientific paradigm of physical and mechanical separation.

53 Dr. Capra's main research interest is theoretical high-energy physics, and he has worked at universities in Paris and California, and at the Imperial College,London.

54 *The Tao of Physics*, p. 130.

55 *The Tao of Physics*, p. 131.

56 *Atomic Physics and the Description of Nature*, p. 57.

57 *On the Intuitive Understanding of Nonlocality as Implied by Quantum Theory*, D. Bohm & B. Hiley in *Foundations of Physics*, vol. 5 (1975), p. 96, 102.

58 *The Synthesis of Yoga* by S. Aurobindo, p. 993.

59 *S-Matrix Interpretation of Quantum Theory* by H. P. Stapp, *Physical Review*, vol. D3 (March 15th, 1971), p. 1303‾20.

60 *Physics and Philosophy*.

61 *The Physicist's Conception of Nature*, p. 244.

62 *Foundations of Tibetan Mysticism*, by Lama Anagarika Govinda, p. 93.

63 The suggestive subtitle to this book is *If the Universe Is the Answer, What Is the Question?*.

64 *The God Particle*, p. 190.

65 This program is published by "Sounds True Recordings" under the title *The Sacred Universe*.

66 In chapter 3, p. 74, of his book *Beyond the Quantum*, Michael Talbot describes the morphic field of a species as a group mind; Sheldrake gives social insects and termites as examples.

67 One can find a detailed account of this event in chapter 3, p. 72–73, of Michael Talbot's *Beyond the Quantum*.

68 From *Ideas and Opinions*.

69 Dr. Wayne Dyer suggests this so eloquently in *The Secrets to Manifesting Your Destiny*.

70 From *Ideas and Opinions*, p. 57.

71 From *Ideas and Opinions*, p. 64.

72 April 20, 1998, p. 57,58.

73 At the end of 1997 The Learning Channel presented "Cyber Warriors," a fascinating program on the evolution and implications of computer technology in the United States.

74 A recent nursing college course offered via TV has been rated "unsatisfactory" in many areas by a majority of students who were enrolled for an entire semester.

75 In *Science, Spirit, and Soul*, Larry Dossey presents new frontiers in mind-body medicine, the subject treated by Deepak
Chopra in *Quantum Healing*.

76 From *Ideas and Opinions*, p. 66.

About the Author

The author was born in 1955 in Romania where he was raised and received his college education in mathematics and computer science. In 1981 he defected from the Communist regime of Romania and spent several months in a political refugee camp in Italy. In 1982 he received his Green Card in order to immigrate into the United States and since then has been teaching mathematics in Austin, Texas, which he finds very rewarding. Over the years he has published several educational articles and has presented at many professional conferences in the United States and Canada. His main interest is the philosophy of general education and the improvement of human life. His extensive research and first hand experience in science, religion, and spirituality led to the writing of this book. Beside family activities and writing, Irie Glajar finds great pleasure in music, traveling, gardening, and sports such as tennis and volleyball.

www.ingramcontent.com/pod-product-compliance
Lightning Source LLC
LaVergne TN
LVHW021447080426
835509LV00018B/2185